The Joy of Giving Homemade Food

illustrations by
LAUREN JARRETT

The Joy of Giving Homemade Food

Unique Homemade Recipes and Creative Packaging Ideas for All Occasions

ANN SERANNE

DAVID McKAY COMPANY, INC.   NEW YORK

Library of Congress Cataloging in Publication Data

Smith, Margaret Ruth, 1914-
   The joy of giving homemade food.

   Includes index.
   1. Cookery. 2. Gifts. I. Title.
TX652.S56   641.5   78-16856
ISBN 0-679-51125-3

10 9 8 7 6 5 4 3 2

Manufactured in the United States of America

DESIGNED BY SALLIE BALDWIN, ANTLER & BALDWIN, INC.

By the same author:

The Art of Egg Cookery
Your Home Freezer
The Complete Book of Home Preserving
The Complete Book of Home Baking
Delectable Desserts
The Complete Book of Desserts
The Epicure's Companion (with John Tebbel)
The Complete Book of Home Freezing
Happy Living (with Evelyn Enright)
Ann Seranne's Good Food and How to Cook It
Ann Seranne's Good Food Without Meat
Ann Seranne's Good Food with a Blender
The Pots and Pans Cookbook (with Joan Wilson)
All About Small Dogs in the Big City

WITH EILEEN GADEN, PHOTOGRAPHER:

The Blender Cookbook
The Best of Near Eastern Cookery
The Church and Club Woman's Companion
The Sandwich Book

COOKBOOKS EDITED BY ANN SERANNE:

America Cooks
The Southern Junior League Cookbook
The Midwestern Junior League Cookbook

Whoever has a heart full of love
Always has something to give

Contents

Introduction

Giving means different things to different people. To some it means buying expensive presents to shower on friends and loved ones; to some it means writing a check or enclosing a crisp new bill in a gift envelope. But to others giving means a bit of himself, a loving thought, a special effort, no matter how small or insignificant that effort might be.

To such people the joy of giving is not limited to the season of peace on earth, good will to men. It is something that continues on in their hearts and is never very far from their minds.

Beginning with New Year's Eve, when champagne corks popping from one end of the globe to another usher in a new year, each month has its holidays and special occasions which bring friends and families together to celebrate, to rejoice, and to feast. But the person who has the joy of giving in his heart can put a holiday flavor into any day of the year. These are the people who have captured the true spirit and meaning of giving.

The home kitchen is a never-ending source of inspiration to the giftgiver. Here in the heart of the home, that Old World custom of creating surprises for family and friends is revived. Here is where the lush berries and fruits of spring and summer are turned into sparkling jams and jellies, where the fragrant herb vinegars are brewed, and where the steaming preserving kettle fills the autumn air with pungent aromas that might easily have come straight out of the *Arabian Nights*.

Here is where cheese spreads are potted in ceramic jars, favorite salad dressings are poured into pretty cruets, salted nuts are packed in glass apothecary jars, wicker baskets are piled high with homemade breads. Here is where the bountiful feasts of the Passover and Easter, of Thanksgiving, Chanukah, and Christmas are prepared and where the fancy cakes, rich candies, and sweet cookies are made for the holiday table and to share with neighbors and friends.

When you share your very own special savory or sweet treats from your home kitchen you know the true meaning of giving. These are gifts that only you can make. These are gifts from the heart.

ANN SERANNE

1

Preserves
with Giving in Mind

The person who knows the difference between buying and giving starts thinking about another year of gifts from the home kitchen as soon as life settles into its everyday routine after the busy holidays of December.

In February and March, citrus fruits are at their most plentiful and best for making into marmalades. Then summer arrives, bringing with it all the wonderful fresh fruits and berries to be made into jams, jellies, and preserves, all of which are far superior to anything that can be purchased in either supermarkets or gourmet shops. No artificial flavors or colors, no chemical additives, just fresh fruit, carefully prepared and naturally preserved in sugar, come out of the preserving kettle with a generous sprinkling of love. And when such homemade preserves are imaginatively packaged in unique containers, they make thoughtful gifts for any occasion throughout the year.

Containers for most preserves may be anything from an empty peanut butter jar or mustard pot to a rare porcelain teacup. But clear containers, either glass or plastic, show off the jewel-like colors of sparkling jellies better than ceramic mugs or earthenware crocks.

When shopping, keep your eyes open for attractive containers in which to package the fragrant produce of your preserving kettle. Standard jelly jars or Mason jars are the most practical containers to use if you plan to ship any of your preserves by parcel post or air freight. But almost any container that may be tightly sealed or resealed can be used for jams and jellies and will travel well if packed and marked "fragile," and supermarket shelves are loaded with such containers in all shapes and sizes. After the contents are used, carefully wash both container and lid, soaking off any labels, and tuck them away on a shelf in a cupboard or closet for later use. Often four or six small jars, each containing a different flavor jam or jelly, make a more attractive gift than one larger jar.

Flea markets and ten-cent stores offer unlimited possibilities of bottles, baskets, wooden bowls, and so on that can be purchased inexpensively and put to good use; and more expensive containers are readily available in drugstores, and gift and hobby shops. Not all need to have reusable lids for fruits preserved in sugar. Unusual containers such as wineglasses, brandy snifters, and glass beakers may be filled with a preserve and sealed against the air by means of a layer of melted paraffin (see page 5 for instructions). The top of the container and the paraffin may be hidden with an attractive cover of gold or silver foil before it is tied with a bright ribbon for gift-giving. Paste or tie on a label neatly printed with the name of the preserve and the cook.

If you are an amateur ceramist (and it's amazing how many good cooks are attracted to the pottery wheel or ceramic studio), you can make your own earthenware or stoneware containers: small crocks, canisters, miniature ginger jars, small pitchers, jugs, soup bowls, even coffee or chocolate cups are all good to use in the packaging of homemade preserves that you plan to carry in-hand for gift-giving. You might fire on a label with the name of the preserve written in gold ink or decorate the container with fruit decals that match the jam or conserve within. The preserve poured into such containers, which do not have airtight lids, must be protected by a layer of paraffin to keep out any airborne molds. Such molds are not harmful or dangerous but will discolor the jam or jelly and alter the flavor.

Use your imagination not only in packaging and labeling but in the preserves themselves. Whenever possible, make your jams and jellies out of the more unusual fruits and berries indigenous to your part of the country— beach plums in New England, rose hips in New Jersey, red haws or crab apples in Pennsylvania, wild grapes in the Connecticut woods, pomegranates and other exotic fruits plentiful in warmer states—to make preserves with a unique flavor that cannot be duplicated in store or supermarket. In other words, make your preserves uniquely yours. And add your own touches to make each jar individual. A few maraschino cherries, whole or chopped, or ½ cup seeded raisins, give a special touch to pale preserves. Add them a couple of minutes before taking the preserve off the heat. Walnut meats, halved or chopped, hickory nuts, or blanched almonds may also be added as you take the kettle from the stove.

Pineapple juice or orange juice substituting for part of the water adds additional flavor to bland fruits such as apples, pears, or peaches. Grated orange or lemon rind or a little freshly ground nutmeg picks up the flavor of many preserves. Mixed spices tied in a bag—cinnamon, ginger, clove, allspice, or a mixture of them all—may be cooked with any preserve. A handful of chopped dried apricots added to a batch of marmalade heightens both flavor and color.

When the syrup surrounding the fruit is clear and thick, it may be flavored with cognac, rum, sherry, Madeira, or port. Like nuts, spirits should be added after the preserve is removed from the heat.

Such personal products stand on their own as thoughtful gifts for any occasion, but you can make them even more special with a little additional thought and inspiration. What could be nicer for mother on Mother's Day or for dad on Father's Day than a large jar of your favorite homemade preserves packaged in a wicker basket or on a tray with a loaf of homemade bread, some sweet rolls, or a dozen homemade brioche.

Any jam, jelly, marmalade, conserve, or canned fruits can be made into a special holiday gift. Brandied cherries, for instance, would be appropriate for George Washington's Birthday. Attach a recipe for Cherries Jubilee and, when delivering your gift, pick up a carton of vanilla ice cream to complete the gesture. Bake a batch of four-leaf-clover-shaped baking powder biscuits or scones and package them on a tray with a jar of your best mint jelly in the center for St. Patrick's Day. Overwrap with transparent film and tie on a big green bow.

Easter might suggest a jar of orange marmalade, a soufflé dish, a wire whisk, and a dozen fresh eggs, all packaged together with a recipe for marmalade soufflé. A visit to your local ceramic shop might uncover a heart-shaped dish for a Valentine gift. Package it with a jar of strawberry preserves and a recipe for a favorite French dessert known as Coeur à la Crème, in which cream cheese is molded in the shape of a heart and garnished with strawberry preserves. Or package the strawberry preserves with a sponge cake baked in an angel food pan and turned out on a glass plate with instructions to surround the cake with fresh strawberries and use the preserves as a glaze. It will serve double duty as both centerpiece and dessert at the Passover feast.

These are but a few special occasion or holiday ideas that come to mind. There are many more ways to combine the produce of your kitchen with "just a little something more" to make gifts that money can't buy. All it takes is a little imagination.

PRESERVES

Every homemaker has her favorite recipes for preserves, so I am only going to give you the basic principles of making each of the different kinds of preserves, then follow these instructions with a few favorites of my own.

HOW TO PRESERVE FRUITS

1. Select firm ripe fruit in perfect condition.
2. Prepare the fruit as you would for the table, slicing large fruit if desired.
3. Work with small quantities of fruit. Several 2-pound batches make a better-quality preserve than one large batch.

4. In a preserving kettle or large saucepan dissolve sugar in water or fruit juice to make a syrup. In general, use an amount of sugar equal to the weight of the fruit itself and 2 cups of water for each pound of sugar. Bring syrup to a boil and boil rapidly for 5 minutes.

5. Drop the fruit into the boiling syrup and cook rapidly over high heat until the fruit is clear and tender. Fast cooking will result in a product that is sparkling and bright. Slow cooking dulls the fruit and darkens the color. At all times the fruit must be well covered with syrup and, if the syrup gets too thick before the fruit is tender, boiling water should be added ½ cup at a time.

6. Continue to boil until a candy thermometer registers 222°, or until syrup is thick.

7. If your preserves are packed hot in clean jars or the fruit is covered with boiling-hot syrup, no further processing is needed. If, however, the preserves are packed cold, it is a wise precaution to process the jars in a water bath. Since the sugar syrup is a preservative in itself, it is only necessary to guard against molds. Processing the jars for 20 minutes in simmering water is all it takes to destroy the molds, which are harmless. An easier method is simply to cover the surface of the preserves with melted paraffin before capping the jars. A small china teapot or jug makes a perfect container in which to melt paraffin. The paraffin must not be too hot, so set the pot into a saucepan of simmering water until it is melted. While the jam, jelly, or conserve is still hot and you've poured it into a Mason jar or gift container, pour a thin layer of paraffin directly on top and let cool. Then add another thin layer, making sure that every bit of the contents is well covered. Two thin layers are more effective than one thicker layer.

BRANDIED CHERRIES OR WHITE GRAPES

Use large white California grapes or dark sweet cherries. Wash, stem, and pit the cherries or wash and cut each grape in half and remove seeds. Cook the pits or seeds in water to cover for 15 minutes and reserve the liquid.

For each 5 cups prepared grapes or cherries, combine 2 cups of the reserved liquid and 2 cups of sugar, bring to a boil, and boil for 5 minutes. Add the fruit and cook rapidly until the grapes or cherries are tender, about 10 minutes. Pack in pint jars and pour ¼ cup cognac or brandy into each jar. Continue to cook the syrup until it is thick, or until it registers 222° on a candy thermometer. Pour the syrup into the jars to overflowing and seal. Store in a dark, cool place.

Makes 2 pint jars.

MÉLANGE DES FRUITS OR RUMTOPH

In France, a mixture of fruits preserved in sugar and brandy is called a Mélange des Fruits. (When rum is used instead of brandy the preserved fruit is known as *rumtoph*.) It is begun each season when homegrown strawberries are at their peak and dark sweet cherries hang in clusters from the trees. Fruit and sugar are combined as the various fruits and berries come into season and brandy is added from time to time. It makes excellent sauce for desserts, hot or cold.

To make it, thoroughly wash a large, wide-mouthed earthenware crock with boiling water and wipe dry. Pour a fifth of good brandy into the crock and add 1 tablespoon mixed whole spices such as clove, allspice, and cinnamon bark, and 1 tablespoon grated lemon, orange, or grapefruit rind.

Hull 1 quart perfect strawberries and add them to the crock along with their weight in sugar. Cover the crock with cheesecloth and let the fruit stand for 1 week in a cool place. Then add 1 quart hulled raspberries and stemmed cherries along with their weight in sugar. Continue to add fruit and sugar as the fruit comes in season. Any or all fruits such as gooseberries, blackberries, peaches, pears, pineapple, plums, and grapes are good. Add more brandy from time to time to keep the fruit covered with liquid at all times. Add additional spices to taste as the crock fills with fruit and syrup.

When the crock is full, place a heavy plate on top of the fruit to keep it submerged in the liquid. Cover with the crock lid. It will not spoil if kept in a cool place. When the fruit has been allowed to mellow, it may be transferred to small ceramic containers for gift-giving.

GINGERED APPLES

Peel and core 5 pounds firm tart apples and cut into wedges. Put apples in a preserving kettle with 3 cups water and cook about 10 minutes, or until just barely fork-tender.

Add 5 pounds sugar, the grated rind of 3 lemons, and ½ cup chopped preserved or candied ginger. Continue to cook until the syrup is thick enough to sheet from a spoon, or until it registers 222° on a candy thermometer.

Ladle into hot jars and seal immediately with either an airtight lid or paraffin.

Makes 4 pints.

BAR-LE-DUC

Wash and stem large red or white currants.

Measure 4 cups currants into a saucepan and pour 1 cup mashed currants over them. Bring the liquid to a boil and simmer for 5 minutes. Add 1½ cups sugar, stir gently, and cook slowly for 5 minutes. Add another 1½ cups sugar and boil rapidly for 5 minutes. Let stand until cold.

Skim out currants and pack them into clean jars. Bring the syrup to a boil again and boil until it jellies, or until it registers 222° on a candy thermometer. Pour the hot, thick syrup over the fruit and seal.

Makes 1 pint.

GOLDEN TOMATO PRESERVES

1 pound yellow pear tomatoes
1½ cups sugar
Juice and grated rind of 1 orange
1 lemon, thinly sliced

Scald tomatoes and slip off the skins, being careful not to crush the fruit. Put the tomatoes and sugar in an enamel bowl, cover tightly, and let stand overnight. In the morning, drain off the juice into heavy saucepan. Add orange juice and rind, and boil until the syrup spins a thread. Add tomatoes and lemon and cook until the tomatoes are clear and the syrup is thick. Pack into hot jars and seal.

Makes 1 pint.

SUN-COOKED STRAWBERRY PRESERVES

If you have never tasted strawberries that have been "cooked" in the sun, you've missed a great taste treat. Each June, as long as the berries are at their peak, I set pan after pan of the preserves on the sun porch. When the berries are plump and deep red in color and the syrup is very thick, I pack them in quart Mason jars for our own use and for family friends who look forward to a fresh batch each summer and never tire of them. For gift-giving I use small porcelain crocks with a lid and a saucer beneath, which can go directly on the breakfast table.

If you don't have a sun porch, set the pans outside in direct sun and cover them with cheesecloth to keep out ants and flying insects. Bring them in at night or if it begins to look like rain.

To make the preserves, put ½ cup hot water in a kettle, add 2 pounds sugar, and bring to a boil, stirring until the sugar is dissolved.

Add 2 pounds cleaned and hulled strawberries and simmer the berries for 2 minutes; they will lose their color and shrink. Pour berries and syrup into large shallow pans and set them in the sun for 3 or 4 days.

When the berries are plump and deep red in color and the syrup is jelled, pack them in clean jars without reheating. Cover with a layer of paraffin to prevent mold from forming on top.

Makes 1 quart.

JAMS

Jam is one of the easiest of all preserves to make and is always a welcome house gift because it is concentrated in its pure fruit flavor without the usual "stretchers" found in commercially prepared jams.

Any edible fruit or berry or a combination can be turned into jam. A few of my favorite flavors are: cranberry/orange, peach/pineapple, peach/plum, pear/apple, pineapple/rhubarb, raspberry/cherry, currant/raspberry, strawberry/gooseberry, elderberry/apple, guava/peach, apricot/pear. But don't you settle for my combos! Make your own kitchen originals.

HOW TO MAKE SPARKLING FRUIT JAM

1. Wash jelly glasses or other glass containers and rinse in boiling water. Set aside upside down to drain and dry.
2. To prepare the fruit, wash, stem, and crush berries; peel, pit, and finely chop or crush whole fruits. Solid-fleshed or underripe fruits should be cooked with a little water in a saucepan with a tight-fitting lid for about 10 minutes, or until soft.
3. Measure fruit into a preserving kettle and bring slowly to a boil. There must be sufficient fruit juice or liquid to keep the fruit from sticking to the bottom of the kettle.
4. Stir in sugar equal to the volume of the fruit or, for a less-sweet jam, three-fourths as much sugar as fruit and, when necessary, 2 tablespoons lemon juice to each pound of fruit.
5. Boil rapidly, stirring constantly, to the jellying point, or to 222° on a candy thermometer.
6. Pour while hot into prepared containers and seal with a thin layer of melted paraffin. Let cool overnight and add a second thin layer of paraffin.
7. Wash the outsides and rims of the glasses and cover with the lids or with aluminum foil.

The following jam recipes do not have yield information because the yield will vary depending on the type and quality of the fruit used. However, once you reach the purée stage, it is possible to determine the yield by using the following formulas:

   2 pounds fruit purée (1 quart) plus 3 cups sugar = 5 8-ounce glasses
   2 pounds fruit purée (1 quart) plus 4 cups sugar = 6 8-ounce glasses

APRICOT/PINEAPPLE JAM

1 pound dried apricots
1 fresh pineapple
Sugar
16 maraschino cherries, halved

Soak the apricots in water to cover until soft. Peel and core the pineapple. Drain the apricots, put apricots and pineapple through a food chopper, saving the juice, and measure fruit and juice.

   In a heavy kettle combine fruit, juice, and ¾ cup sugar for each cup prepared fruit; stir until the sugar is dissolved. Add the cherries and bring to a boil. Cook over low heat for 25–30 minutes, or until the fruit is clear and the jam is thick, stirring occasionally. Pour into hot jars and seal.

BLUEBERRY/CURRANT JAM

   Put 1 quart blueberries, washed and drained, through a food chopper. Add 1 cup water, bring to a boil, and cook for 6 minutes.

   Wash 1 pint currants and, without removing the berries from the stems, cook them with 1 cup water very slowly in a covered saucepan for 8 minutes. Press the currant pulp and juice through a fine sieve to remove stems and seeds.

   Mix the currant pulp and the cooked blueberries, bring to a boil, and cook for 5 minutes. Add 3 cups sugar and boil rapidly until the jam is thick enough to sheet from the edge of the spoon. Pour into sterilized jars and seal while hot.

MIXED FRUIT JAM

2 lemons   *6 pears*
2 oranges   *6 peaches*
6 apples   *Sugar*

Slice the lemons and oranges thinly, cover them with cold water, and let stand overnight. In the morning, bring the water to a boil and simmer the lemons and oranges for 10 minutes.

Peel and core the apples and pears; peel and pit the peaches. Dice the fruit and measure. Add the fruit and an equal amount of sugar to the oranges and lemons, bring to a boil, and cook until the jam is thick. Pour into hot jars and seal.

SWEET AND SOUR PEPPER JAM

12 *large red peppers*
1 *tablespoon salt*
1½ *pounds sugar*
2 *cups vinegar*

Stem and seed the peppers and chop the flesh finely. Sprinkle the peppers with the salt, let stand 3–4 hours, and rinse in cold water. Put the peppers in a preserving kettle with the sugar and vinegar, bring to a boil, and simmer until the jam is thick, stirring frequently. Pour into jars and seal.

This jam is delicious served with cream cheese.

ROSE HIP JAM

Gather rose hips before they grow soft and cut off the heads and stems. Slit the hips in half and discard the seeds and pithy flesh. Cover the hips with water, cook until soft, and press through a sieve. Measure the purée.

To each 4 cups rose hip purée add 1 cup peeled and finely chopped tart apple and, if desired, a handful of chopped fresh red or pink rose petals.

Slice 1 lemon thinly and cook it in ½ cup water for 15 minutes. Drain the liquid into the rose hip purée. Add 5 cups sugar, bring to a boil, and cook slowly until thick. Pour into jars and seal.

CONSERVES

Conserves are made in exactly the same way as jams. The distinguishing feature of a conserve is that it is always a blend of two or more kinds of fruit. It usually contains thin slices of citrus fruit or juice and often raisins or nut meats or both. Small fruits and berries are often left whole but large fruits are sliced or chopped. The prepared fruit is measured and mixed with three-fourths the volume of sugar. It is then cooked until it is thick but still slightly runny. The nuts are added during the last few moments of cooking.

Here are a handful of typical conserve recipes that may inspire you to your own combinations of fruit and nuts.

CANTALOUPE/PEACH CONSERVE

4 cups chopped cantaloupe   ½ teaspoon nutmeg
4 cups chopped peaches   ¼ teaspoon salt
6 cups sugar   1 teaspoon grated orange peel
4 tablespoons lemon juice   ½ cup blanched almonds

Mix the cantaloupe and peaches and bring to a boil. Add the sugar and
lemon juice and cook until the conserve is thick. Add the nutmeg, salt, orange
peel, and almonds and continue to cook for 3 minutes longer. Pour into hot
jars and seal.

BLACK CHERRY/ORANGE CONSERVE

2 oranges   ¼ cup lemon juice
4 cups pitted sweet black cherries   ¾ cup shredded blanched almonds
3½ cups sugar

Wash and slice the oranges thinly. Cover the slices with cold water, bring to
a boil, and cook until soft. Add the cherries, sugar, and lemon juice and continue to boil until the conserve is thick and clear. Add the nuts and cook for
2 minutes. Pour into hot jars and seal.

APPLE/CHERRY/PINEAPPLE CONSERVE

3 cups chopped apples   11 cups sugar
8 cups pitted cherries   ½ teaspoon salt
2 cups chopped pineapple   1 cup shelled nuts

Mix the fruit and sugar and let stand for 4–5 hours. Bring the mixture to a
boil and boil until the conserve is thick. Add the salt and nuts 5 minutes
before cooking is finished. Pour into hot jars and seal.

BLUEBERRY CONSERVE

2 cups water   ½ orange, thinly sliced
4 cups sugar   ½ cup raisins
½ lemon, thinly sliced   4 cups blueberries

Bring the water and sugar to a boil. Add the lemon, orange, and raisins and
simmer for 5 minutes. Add the blueberries and cook gently until the con-

serve is quite thick, stirring frequently but being careful not to crush the berries. Pour into hot jars and seal.

CRANBERRY CONSERVE

Grated peel and pulp of 2 oranges　*1 cup raisins*
2 cups water　*¼ teaspoon salt*
4 cups cranberries　*½ cup chopped nut meats*
3 cups sugar

Cook the orange peel and pulp in the water for 20 minutes. Add the cranberries, sugar, raisins, and salt and boil rapidly until the jellying point. Add the nut meats and cook for 5 minutes longer. Pour into hot jars and seal.

PINEAPPLE/STRAWBERRY/CHERRY CONSERVE

1 quart strawberries　*2 cups chopped pineapple*
1 quart cherries　*Sugar*
1 orange

Wash and hull the berries. Wash, stem, and pit the cherries. Slice the orange very thinly or put through a food chopper. Combine all the fruits and weigh. Add an equal weight of sugar and bring to a boil. Cook slowly until the mixture is thick and clear. Pour into hot jars and seal.

Delicious with cream cheese.

JELLIES AND MARMALADES

No other kind of preserve is as enthusiastically received or as rewarding to make as a pure marmalade or jelly.

A perfect jelly captures the full flavor of the fruit in a clear, transparent, tender jell. A marmalade has the same jelly base but holds in suspension thin slivers of fruit or peel.

Not all fruits and berries lend themselves to perfect jelly. Such fruits as strawberries, peaches, cherries, and pears contain little or no natural pectin and must be combined with such fruits as red currants, gooseberries, or apples, which are high in pectin, or commercial pectin must be added.

Adding commercial pectin is the quick, easy, and sure method of making jelly, but when you add pectin you are diluting the flavor and the jelly will resemble much more closely the commercially prepared products. Maybe this suits your needs and, if so, all you have to do is follow the directions on the bottle of pectin.

I'm going to give you old-fashioned recipes that are tried and true, ones that are far superior to any diluted product because they extract the pectin directly from the fruit along with its juice and flavor.

But first, a list of fruits and fruit combinations that make excellent jelly without the addition of pectin.

FRUITS AND COMBINATIONS THAT MAKE EXCELLENT JELLY

Apple
Apple and Strawberry
Apricot and Plum
Blackberry
Crab Apple
Crab Apple and Cherry
Crab Apple and Raspberry
Currant
Currant and Apple
Currant and Apricot
Currant and Pear
Currant, Peach, and Pineapple
Fig and Lemon
Grape
Grape and Apple
Grape and Apricot
Grape and Orange
Grapefruit
Grapefruit and Cherry
Lemon

Lemon and Cherry
Lemon and Raspberry
Loganberry
Loganberry and Pineapple
Orange
Orange and Apple
Orange and Pineapple
Orange and Plum
Peach and Lemon
Peach and Apple
Peach and Quince
Plum
Plum and Raspberry
Quince
Quince and Apple
Quince and Apricot
Quince and Pineapple
Raspberry
Raspberry and Currant
Roselle

HOW TO MAKE HOMEMADE JELLIES AND MARMALADES

1. Select fruits from the above list. Wash, drain, hull, and stem as needed. It is not necessary to peel, core, or seed the fruit as these will be discarded after the juice is extracted. Cut hard fruits into pieces. Crush soft fruits and berries.

2. Put no more than 2 quarts prepared fruit into a preserving kettle. Add from 1 to 2 cups water to each pound of hard fruits. Add 4 cups water to

each pound of citrus fruits. Juice fruits such as currants, berries, and grapes need no added liquid.

3. Bring fruit and liquid to a boil and boil rapidly until the fruit is just tender. Do not overcook or you may reduce the jellying qualities of the juice.

4. Pour the hot cooked fruit into jelly bag suspended over a bowl or use four layers of cheesecloth stretched and tied over the top of a deep pan and let the juice drip into the container beneath. Let the juice drip overnight without disturbing the bag or cheesecloth.

  IN GENERAL: 1 pound juicy fruit will make 1 cup of juice

  1 cup juice and ¾ cup sugar will make 1 cup jelly

5. Measure the juice and sugar into a saucepan and bring to a boil, stirring until the sugar is dissolved. Then boil rapidly until two drops on the side of a spoon run together and slide or sheet off the spoon, or until it registers 222° on a candy thermometer.

6. Remove jelly from the heat and skim the surface if necessary. Pour into clean jars and let cool and set.

7. With a damp cloth remove any jelly that may be on the jar and cover with a layer of melted paraffin.

8. Cover the paraffin with a lid or aluminum foil, label attractively, and store in a cool, dry place.

APPLE/GERANIUM JELLY

Use hard-ripe tart apples. Wash the apples and discard stems and blossom ends. Slice fruit into a kettle and add water to barely cover (2 cups water to 4 cups fruit). Bring water to a boil and simmer until fruit is soft. Turn fruit and juice into a jelly bag and let the juice drip into a container placed below.

Measure the juice and bring to a rolling boil. Add ¾ cup sugar to each cup of juice and stir until sugar is dissolved. Then boil rapidly until the jellying point is reached.

Put a rose geranium leaf in the bottom of each jelly jar. Skim the jelly and fill the jars.

GRAPE JELLY

Wash, stem, and crush grapes. Add a small amount of water, bring to a boil, and simmer for 15 minutes. Strain the juice through a jelly bag and let the juice stand overnight in a cool place to let any formation of tartaric acid crystals settle to the sides and bottom of the container. In the morning, pour the juice carefully off the sediment in the bottom, measure, and bring to a boil. For each cup of juice add ¾ cup sugar and boil rapidly to the jellying point.

QUINCE/ORANGE JELLY

Wash and quarter quinces and discard the cores. Barely cover the fruit with water, bring to a boil, and simmer for about 45 minutes, or until the fruit is tender. Strain the juice through a jelly bag, measure, and add an equal amount of orange juice and a little of the grated rind. Bring the juice to a boil and simmer for 20 minutes. Stir in ¾ cup sugar for each cup of the combined juices and boil rapidly to the jellying point.

RASPBERRY/CURRANT JELLY

Wash 4 quarts each of red raspberries and red currants. Put them in a preserving kettle and mash well. Bring the juice to a boil and simmer the fruit for 30 minutes. Strain the juice through a jelly bag. Measure the juice and bring to a boil. Boil rapidly for 5 minutes, stir in 1 cup sugar for each cup of juice, and continue boiling rapidly for about 5 minutes longer, or to the jellying point.

STRAWBERRY/RHUBARB JELLY

Wash and chop 1 pound pink rhubarb and add just enough water to keep it from burning. Add the juice and grated rind of 1 lemon and 1 orange, bring to a boil, and simmer until the rhubarb is tender. Add 1 quart hulled strawberries and simmer for 10 minutes longer. Strain the juice through a jelly bag. Measure the juice and bring to a boil. Stir in 1 cup sugar for each cup juice and boil rapidly until the jellying point.

LEMON MARMALADE

4 cups thinly sliced, seeded lemons
3 quarts water
9 cups sugar

Put the lemon slices and water in a preserving kettle, bring to a boil, and cook rapidly for about 20 minutes, or until the lemon rind is tender. Drain and measure the liquid. Add enough water to make 3 quarts of liquid, return the liquid and the lemons to the kettle, and stir in the sugar. Bring to a boil again and cook rapidly until the mixture sheets from a spoon, or registers 222° on a candy thermometer.

LIME MARMALADE

Follow directions for Lemon Marmalade, using 3 cups sliced limes and 1 cup sliced lemons.

GREEN GRAPE MARMALADE

4 cups young green Concord grapes
1 cup water
4 cups sugar
Juice of 1 lemon

Wash and stem the grapes. Any large grapes should be halved and the seeds discarded. Add the water, bring to a boil, and simmer until the grapes are tender. Add sugar and boil to the jellying point. Add lemon juice and boil for 5 minutes longer.

BITTER ORANGE MARMALADE

Weigh a preserving kettle. Cut 6 bitter oranges in half, squeeze out the juice and seeds, and strain the juice into the kettle. Put the seeds into a small bowl, just cover them with warm water, and let stand overnight. With kitchen scissors, cut the orange peel into fine slivers along with any bits of pulp adhering to it. Add the peel to the juice and weigh kettle again, subtracting its original empty weight to get the weight of juice and peel. Add 3 cups water for every pound of juice and peel and let stand overnight.

In the morning, drain all the jelly off the seeds into the kettle. Bring the mixture in the kettle to a boil and simmer for 2 hours. Do not boil hard or too much moisture will be evaporated.

Weigh the kettle again and subtract its original empty weight to get the weight of juice and peel. To every pound of juice and peel add 1 pound sugar. Bring again to a boil and boil rapidly for about 30 minutes to the jellying point, or until a candy thermometer registers 222°.

WILD CHERRY MARMALADE

2 oranges
1 quart pitted wild cherries
4 tablespoons lemon juice
3½ cups sugar

Peel the oranges, discard the white membrane from the peel, and cut the peel into slivers. Cut the orange pulp into small pieces, mix with the rind, and measure. Add an equal measure of water, bring to a boil, and simmer until the rind is tender. Add the cherries, lemon juice, and sugar and cook rapidly until the jellying point.

GINGERED PEAR HONEY

5 cups finely chopped or ground
    fresh pears
1 cup canned crushed pineapple

5 cups sugar
Juice and grated rind of 1 lime
1 tablespoon ground ginger

Combine all ingredients in heavy saucepan. Bring to a boil and cook over low heat for 35–40 minutes, stirring constantly, until fruit is transparent and liquid is thick.

2

Gifts from the Herb Garden from a Cook with a Green Thumb

HERB GARDENS, JELLIES, VINEGARS, AND SPREADS

You really do not need a green thumb to grow herbs. Most of them thrive in average soil providing they get plenty of sunshine and water, and they require a minimum of care.

If you have no limitations on the size of your herb garden or where you place it, choose a sunny spot as close to the kitchen door as possible and near a hose outlet. Whether it's the proximity to the house or because wild animals do not care for the pungent flavor of herbs, I do not know, but with the exception of an occasional chipmunk that seeks refuge from the cat under the shade of a large rhubarb leaf, none has ever bothered mine. And it's not because we don't have plenty of four-footed creatures on the property.

Nor do herbs seem susceptible to pests with the exception of the aphids that at certain seasons of the year seem to rise in cloud formation from the mint and sorrel patches. A rough hosing usually takes care of them, but if they survive the dousing, a bucket full of salty or soapy water gets rid of them without harming the herbs.

If your herb garden is to look neat and cared for, some rather simple rules should be observed and your plot of ground should be intelligently planted. You'll need to know which herbs are annuals, which are biennials, which are perennials, and how tall each is likely to grow. If you back the plot up against a fence or the wall of the house or porch, you can put it to good advantage by setting trellises against it or use the fence itself for climbing vegetables such as snow peas, cherry tomatoes, cucumbers, or pole beans. You can also plant a few of the herbs that grow tall, like lovage or sweet cicely, and, of course, the birds will love it if you tuck in a few sunflower seeds.

If your garden plot is large, it is best to divide it into smaller plots by means of gravel or flagstone walks. Place a birdbath or a sundial in the center and plant a variety of the creeping thymes around it.

If you are limited in space, you will have to forget about aromatic herbs such as lemon verbena, rose geranium, mignonette, and lavender, which are used mainly for their fragrance in sachets or potpourris, and the tisanes used in teas such as chamomile and catnip. You'll have to concentrate on the thirteen most popular herbs used in the kitchen. These are:

tarragon	marjoram	mint	sweet basil
oregano	thyme	sage	dill
savory	rosemary	chives	chervil
			parsley

Of these, tarragon, oregano, savory, marjoram, thyme, rosemary, mint, sage, and chives are perennials. The others are annuals or biennials but should be treated like annuals.

You will get faster and better results with all of these if you start them from nursery plants or greenhouse seedlings. However, dill, parsley, chervil, and sweet basil may be successfully grown from seed as soon as danger of frost is past. After the seedlings have reached a couple of inches in height, they should be thinned and the tender thinnings added to your green salads. All of them grow best in slightly acid soil.

When only a small amount of land is available for an herb garden, you will have to be more innovative in planning and designing the space, and you may wish to include in that space some salad greens along with the herbs. A good selection can be grown within the confines of a circle no more than 8–10 feet in diameter.

Choose a sunny spot as close to the kitchen as possible and plant a large clump of tarragon in the center in place of the sundial or birdbath in the larger garden. From this, set four circles of plants about 1 foot apart, beginning with those herbs that grow tallest and ending with small border plants around the outer periphery. For the first circle around the tarragon, and 1 foot from it, plant sweet basil, summer savory, sweet marjoram, and chives. A nice combination for the second row might be a selection of lettuce plants —some loose head varieties such as butter crunch, bibb, and Boston and some leaf varieties such as oak leaf. Between the lettuce plants sprinkle some seeds of burnet; as the lettuce is pulled the burnet plants will fill in the spaces.

In the third row out from the tarragon, plant curly garden cress and roquette, which can be followed in warmer months with curly endive or corn salad. Parsley and chervil mixed with radish seeds make an excellent outer border row. The radishes will be ready to eat before the parsley begins to show. When the parsley seedlings are a couple of inches high, thin the plants to stand about 6 inches apart and add the sprouts to your evening salad.

Where there is no room for a garden, some herbs may be successfully grown as hedges, as lawn borders, and in rock gardens; others take well to window boxes, redwood tubs, large clay pots, or even hanging baskets.

Herbs that grow well as edgings or in rock gardens are curly parsley, chervil, chives, sweet woodruff, purple or dwarf basil, any of the thyme family such as garden thyme, mother of thyme, lemon thyme, or caraway thyme, winter savory, borage, sweet marjoram, oregano, and chamomile.

Popular culinary herbs such as sage and rosemary, and the lesser-known hyssop are types of almost evergreen shrubs with aromatic leaves and winter well. Rosemary must be potted and stored in cold frames. Hyssop, planted from seed, will grow a foot high during the first year, and plants should be thinned to about 12 inches. It can be clipped like a box hedge at the expense of its blossoms.

A couple of perennial aromatic herbs, used mostly in sachets and pot-pourri, also make excellent hedges. Rue is a perennial that grows well from seed and transplants easily. Its lacy foliage grows about 2 feet high and, if not clipped, bears small bright yellow blossoms. Lavender is one of the most fragrant and beautiful hedge herbs. It also grows about 2 feet high and may be trimmed if desired.

Herbs that grow well in window boxes are sage, chives, parsley, chervil, rose geranium, and miniature plants of rosemary, oregano, basil, and garden thyme.

GIFTS THAT GROW

SEEDLING BASKET

If you are an herb enthusiast, a delightful gift for friends who like to cook is a fruit basket filled with tiny clay or peat pots, each containing a different seedling such as basil, thyme, parsley, oregano, chives, and tarragon. Cover the basket with a blanket of fresh thyme and tie a flower and herb nosegay or tuzzie-muzzie on the handle with a gay ribbon.

Tuzzie-Muzzies: Tuzzie-muzzies are small, old-fashioned herb bouquets. They are meant to be held in the hand, for the warmth increases their fragrance. Each flower in the nosegay has a sentimental meaning—violets in the center for loyalty, surrounded by heliotropes for eternal love, surrounded by marjoram for happiness, thyme for courage, or rosemary for remembrance.

MINIATURE HERB GARDENS

The thin wooden boxes that wheels of cheese are shipped in, or oval Shaker pantry boxes crafted from thin maple, can be gathered from local markets and can be made into charming miniature herb garden gifts. They vary in size from 6 inches to about 16 inches in diameter and 6½ inches deep, and they can be stained or painted or decoupaged.

To transform the box into a container for herbs, drill a circle of holes, about ½ inch in diameter, in the bottom of the box for drainage, keeping them 2 inches from the outer edges. The boxes can be painted with Bondex or Curpinol, according to package directions, or can be decorated with decals, wallpaper, decorative wrapping paper, etc. Shellac the decorations well as protection against dampness and rain. Scatter stones or rubble over the bottom of the box, spread with a layer of sand, and fill with a good potting soil.

In the larger boxes, a variety of herbs can be planted such as rosemary, garden thyme, sweet marjoram, sweet basil, winter savory, and chives. Plant the one that grows tallest in the center, leaving plenty of room between the plants for the herbs to grow.

Attach a small tag to each plant to identify it and include an instruction sheet for the recipient. Instructions for the care of the herb garden should read:

"With loving care, these newly potted plants will have established good roots in about a month. Set your miniature herb garden on small cleats, to allow proper drainage, in full sun but against a wall or under the edge of an awning, where it will have shade part of the time. Water each day, more often if the weather is extremely hot and dry. After one month, feed the plants once a week with a liquid plant food, carefully following manufacturer's directions for use."

These make great gifts for Mother's Day or for a spring housewarming.

GARDEN HERBS

Name	Type	Height	Uses
Basil	Annual	2–2½ feet	Good with all tomato dishes in salads, spaghetti sauces, vinegars and oils, and with cream cheese and vegetables.

Name	*Type*	*Height*	*Uses*
Borage	Annual	2 feet	Used in salads, beverages, with wild game, chicken, or vegetables.
Burnet	Perennial	1–2 feet	Used in salads, beverages, vinegars and teas.
Chervil	Annual or Biennial	18 inches	Used as a garnish on almost anything, especially salads, omelets, and fish. One of the herbs used in an herb bouquet.
Chives	Perennial	8–10 inches	Used as a garnish, especially for hamburgers, soups, salads, savory butters, and cheese spreads.
Caraway	Self-seeding	2 feet	Leaves are used in soups and salads; the seeds in soups, meat stews, sauerkraut dishes, breads, cakes, and with vegetables.
Coriander	Annual	10–12 inches	Leaves are known as Chinese parsley, or cilantro. It has a strange, pungent odor and flavor. Use like parsley. The seeds are used in cheese spreads, with fruit, in pickles, salads, soups, and cookies.
Catnip	Perennial	2 feet	Used for tea and as a tonic for cats.
Costmary	Perennial	3–4 feet	Used in salads, cakes, meats, poultry, game, and as an herb tea.
Cumin	Annual	2 feet	Seeds are used in appetizers, Mexican dishes, breads, cookies, fruit pies, and with cheese and eggs. It is one of the ingredients in curry powder.
Dill	Annual	18 inches	Used as a garnish for almost anything: cucumbers, soups and sauces, tomato dishes, potato dishes, and in cottage cheese, cole slaw, pickles, and vinegars.
Fennel	Annual	2 feet	Leaves are good with fish, in salads and soups. Seeds are good

Name	Type	Height	Uses
			with cheese, fish, and vegetable dishes.
Hyssop	Perennial	2 feet	Used in stews and soups and with fruit cocktails.
Lemon Balm	Perennial	2 feet	Used in fish dishes, desserts, soups and salads, and as a flavoring for wine punches and teas.
Lemon Verbena	Perennial	2 feet	Used in sachets and potpourris.
Lavender	Perennial	3 feet	Used primarily as a perfume in sachets and potpourris, but good in jellies and to flavor wine beverages.
Lovage	Perennial	5–7 feet	The tender leaves may be used like celery, in soups and salads and to flavor chowders, sauces, and stews.
Marjoram	Annual	6 inches	Used in tomato dishes and sauces, soups, stuffings, stews, vegetables, eggs, and cheese.
Oregano	Perennial	2 feet	A must in Italian dishes, pizza, and spaghetti sauces; also good in meat loaves, stews, pork, and chicken dishes.
Parsley	Biennial	10 inches	Used as a garnish for almost anything. Also used in soups, stews, chowders, and herb bouquets.
Rosemary	Perennial	4 feet	Used for pork and lamb, beef or veal, in stews and chicken sautées.
Rue	Perennial	2 feet	A pungent herb to use sparingly in cheese dishes, vegetable dishes, tomato juice cocktails, salads, and perfumes.
Sage	Perennial	2–3 feet	Used for sausages and stuffings, also good with veal dishes and in anything made from dried beans, peas, or lentils. Good with creamed vegetables.

Name	Type	Height	Uses
Savory	Perennial	12–15 inches	Used for vegetables and fish, in meat and fish stews, in stuffings, meat and chicken loaves and balls.
Sorrel	Perennial	2–3 feet	Use shredded in chicken broth for one of the world's greatest soups, as a bed for cooking fish, and in bean soups.
Sweet Cicely	Perennial	3 feet	Used for sachets and potpourris.
Sweet Woodruff	Perennial	3 feet	Used for May wine and champagne punches.
Spearmint	Perennial	12 inches	Used in fruit appetizers, lamb sauces, salads, and as a garnish for mint juleps.
Tarragon	Perennial	2 feet	Used for veal, chicken, fish, stew, soup, sauces, eggs, and in vinegars. One of the herbs used in an herb bouquet.
Thyme	Perennial	4 inches	Used for beef stews, in stuffings and scalloped vegetables, in meat loaves and balls. One of the herbs used in an herb bouquet.
Tansy	Perennial	2–3 feet	Primarily used for sachets and perfumes, but may be used sparingly with fish, in omelets and meat pies. Makes a good herb tea.

NOTE: Most of the perennial herbs weather well in northern climates providing they are well mulched for winter. The exceptions are rosemary and lemon verbena. These should be transferred to pots and stored in a cool place until spring.

More practical herb gifts than the live seedlings and miniature herb gardens are herb jellies, canapé spreads, flavorful butters, and vinegars made from fresh or dried herbs and packaged in attractive pharmaceutical flasks, apothecary jars, or small ceramic canisters, each bearing the name of the herb within. Less expensive grocery store jars and bottles will need some glamorous labels or attached recipe tags.

You might prefer to combine several herbs in little cheesecloth bags to be used for teas or to flavor soups and stews.

The imaginative ways to use and package herbs for gift-giving are endless, and it would be impossible to give you directions for all of them within the confines of one chapter of a book. I am, however, going to pass along the herb gifts that appeal to me the most.

HERB JELLIES

BASIC HERB JELLY

Herb jellies are made with a base of tart apple juice. Bring the apple juice to a boil and stir in ¾ cup sugar for each cup juice. Add a large handful of herbs such as lemon verbena, sage, bay leaves, tarragon, sweet basil, thyme, or marjoram and cook the juice rapidly for about 15 minutes, or until the jelly sheets from the edge of the spoon (222°).

Strain out the herbs. Place a fresh herb leaf in the bottom of each glass and fill with the hot jelly. Cover with two thin layers of melted paraffin.

MINT JELLY

1 cup boiling water
1 cup firmly packed shredded mint leaves
Apple juice
Sugar
Whole mint leaves

Pour the boiling water over the shredded mint leaves and let stand for 1 hour. Press the juice from the leaves and set aside.

To each cup of apple juice add 2 tablespoons of the mint liquid and bring to a boil. Add ¾ cup sugar for each cup of apple juice and boil rapidly to the jellying point. Put a few fresh mint leaves into each jar and fill with the hot jelly. Cool and cover with two thin layers of melted paraffin.

HERB VINEGARS

There are many types of vinegars; the most common are pure cider, white distilled, red wine, or white wine. Less common ones are flavored with lemon, tomato, pimiento, raspberries or strawberries, peaches or pears, and from these a variety of flavored vinegars may be made.

Garlic- and shallot-flavored vinegars and those infused with the essence of such herbs as tarragon, sweet basil, marjoram, and dill are ideal to add variety to salads or a special zest to sauces or marinades. Occasionally vinegars are flavored with spices or a combination of herbs and spices.

Your very own special combination of flavored vinegars make marvelous gifts, especially for city friends who have no access to fresh herbs and must depend on the commercially dried ones. You will need to start saving all kinds of bottles—old wine bottles, empty maple syrup, or apple cider jugs—in which to package your vinegars. If you are going to buy your herbs from a local vegetable stand or farmer you may want to settle for the small bottles with resealable caps that many fruit juices and most soft drinks are sold in today. On the other hand, if you have your own lush herb garden you can afford to be more generous and will tuck away empty pint, quart, and half-gallon bottles and jugs for your vinegars. Vinegar is relatively inexpensive, and the herbs cost little more than your time spent to keep down the weeds.

For more prestigious gifts you might make the rounds of antique shops in search of old, rare bottles with crystal or porcelain stoppers. Such bottles filled with your own aromatic vinegar would be welcomed by even the most important people on your gift-giving list.

If you are handy with the sewing machine you can make carry-all bags or drawstring pouches of velvet, imitation suede, plastic-lined canvas, and so on and pack in each a bottle of your homemade herb vinegar, a bottle of imported French olive oil, and a jar of coarsely cracked pepper.

For bottles that have no stoppers or reusable tops, you can buy corks at your local hardware store in any number of sizes to fit. To transform these into bottles with the look of a gift, invert the filled and corked bottle into a small pan of hot sealing wax, letting the wax flow over both the cork and the rim of the bottle. This adds just the right finish to the bottle and insures against leakage.

Some herb vinegars need to be filtered, and an easy way to do this is to put your Chemex coffee maker to work. If you don't have a Chemex and expect to be making a lot of vinegars, it might be a good idea to buy a pint-sized one and an extra box of the small filter papers.

HERB VINEGAR

There are two popular methods of making herb vinegar—the hot method and the cold.

For my own use, I simply pack a wide-mouthed gallon jar or crock as full as possible with fresh tarragon or dill, cover it with cider or distilled vinegar, and let it stand until I am ready to use it. The herb remains in the container until the very last drop of vinegar is used.

For gift-giving, I put a few perfect sprigs of the herb into a glass bottle and fill it with the herb vinegar from my larger container. After the bottles are filled, I dip the lids into melted red sealing wax, tie labels around the necks with a red ribbon, and attach a note suggesting that the recipient fill the bottle to the top with plain vinegar after half of it has been used.

MIXED HERB VINEGAR

Put into a quart jar 1 tablespoon each chopped mint leaves, tarragon leaves, fresh chervil, and marjoram. Add 6 tablespoons chopped chives or green onions, 1 small bay leaf, and 2 cloves. Fill the jar with vinegar and let stand for 1 week. Then strain through flannel or filter through filter paper. Bottle, seal, and label.

MINT VINEGAR

This should be made just before the plants come into blossom in August and is great to use in fruit salads.

Fill a jar with clean mint leaves and add enough wine vinegar to cover the mint. Cover the jar tightly with heavy waxed paper inside the aluminum or metal cover. Let the mint leaves remain in the vinegar until all the vinegar has been used.

BASIL VINEGAR

The hot vinegar method results in the best-flavored basil vinegar, especially good on sliced fresh tomatoes or used in a French or vinaigrette sauce for tomato salads.

Pick the basil in the cool of the morning. Crush the leaves a bit and pack them into a quart jar. Fill the jar with boiling-hot vinegar. Seal the jar and let it stand for 2 weeks, shaking it each day. Strain the vinegar through flannel or filter it through filter paper and pour into clean bottles. Cork or cap the containers and store in a dark, cool place.

For gift-giving, add a sprig of the fresh herb to each bottle before corking it.

FRUITY SALAD VINEGAR

Three flavors that, tempered by vinegar, blend together subtly to make a delicious, fruity salad vinegar are garlic, dill, and fresh mint.

Drop 2 or 3 peeled cloves of garlic into a quart glass bottle of cider vinegar. Add 3 heads of fresh dill and a handful of whole mint stalks.

Place the bottle in a sunny window and let the garlic and herbs steep in the vinegar for 3 weeks. Strain off or remove from the windowsill to a cool place until ready to use or rebottle.

PEPPERY VINEGAR

Put into a quart jar 4 dozen hot red peppers about 1 inch long. Fill the jar with vinegar and seal. Let the jar stand in a warm place for 2 weeks, shaking the jar every day. Strain, bottle, seal, and store.

SPICED RED WINE VINEGAR

To 1 quart red wine vinegar add ½ teaspoon each of grated lemon peel, mace, dry mustard, cinnamon, cloves, white mustard seeds, black mustard seeds, onion salt, thyme, black pepper, and paprika, plus 1 teaspoon celery salt, 1 clove garlic, ½ teaspoon cayenne, and 2 bay leaves. Bring the vinegar to a boil; cool and strain through filter paper or flannel into a china bowl. Cover the bowl with a clean cloth and let the vinegar stand for 3 days. Again filter or strain the vinegar, pour into sterilized bottles, and seal.

TARRAGON VINEGAR

Pack a quart Mason jar loosely with sprays of fresh tarragon and fill the jar with vinegar. Let stand in a dark place for 10 days. Strain or filter the vinegar, pour into sterilized bottles or jars, and cork or cap. Store in a cool, dark place.

MINT VINEGAR FOR SAUCES

Mix 2 cups shredded young spearmint leaves with 1 cup sugar and let stand for 5 minutes. Bring to a boil 1 quart fruit vinegar. Add the sugar and spearmint and stir, crushing the leaves against the side of the pan. Simmer for 3 minutes and strain the vinegar through flannel or filter it through filter paper. Bottle and let ripen for several weeks before using.

SWEET, SPICED VINEGAR FOR FRUIT SALADS

To 1 quart vinegar add 2 cups sugar, 1 tablespoon each of chopped cinnamon sticks and white mustard seeds, 1 teaspoon each of allspice, cloves, thyme leaves, and salt, and 4 bay leaves. Bring the vinegar to a boil, then pour it over a lime or lemon, thinly sliced. Strain or filter the juice, bottle in sterilized bottles or jars, and cork or cap. Store in a dark, cool place.

GARLIC VINEGAR

Crush 3 large cloves garlic, add 1 quart vinegar, and mix well. Let stand, covered, in the refrigerator for 2 days, then filter or strain, pour into sterilized bottles, and store in a dark, dry place.

RAVIGOTE VINEGAR

Combine 1 teaspoon each of fresh tarragon leaves, chives, and shallots, all finely chopped, ⅓ teaspoon each of grated lemon rind and onion, and 1 clove garlic, mashed. Add 1 quart vinegar and 1 tablespoon brandy and let stand in a warm place for 2 weeks. Filter, bottle, seal, or cork and store in a cool, dark, dry place.

HERB SPREADS

These are nice to keep in the refrigerator for ready use. For gift-giving, pack them into mustard jars or ceramic crocks and cover tightly.

Dill Butter: Cream 1 cup sweet butter with 1 teaspoon lemon juice. Fold in 4 tablespoons chopped dill. Pack into an 8-inch crock and use on broiled fish, veal scallops, or sautéed chicken breasts.

Rosemary Butter: Use rosemary in place of dill and serve with broiled lamb chops or rack of spring lamb.

Chive Butter: Use chopped chives in place of dill. Use on poached chicken.

Tarragon Butter: Use chopped tarragon in place of dill. Use on almost any fish, meat, or fowl.

Herb Butter Canapé Spread: One of the nicest canapé spreads to use at home or to take along as a gift is simply made by creaming sweet butter with chopped fresh herbs of your choice, perhaps some sweet basil or marjoram or chives. Spread this on thin fingers of homemade brioche.

For gift-giving, pack it in small ceramic soufflé dishes or custard cups and wrap gold aluminum over the tops with a bright ribbon. Attach a "how-to-use" label and store in the refrigerator until ready to take to a friend.

GARLIC MUSTARD

2 large onions, sliced   ½ teaspoon red pepper
4 cloves garlic, thinly sliced   2 tablespoons sugar
2 cups vinegar   1 cup dry mustard
2 teaspoons salt

Peel and crush the onions and garlic lightly and then put onion, garlic, and vinegar in a clean jar. Cover and let stand in refrigerator for 24 hours. Pour off liquid and reserve; discard onions and garlic.

Combine salt, pepper, sugar, and mustard. Gradually stir in ½ cup of the reserved vinegar. Bring remaining reserved vinegar to a boil. Gradually add to the mustard mixture. Bring to a boil and cook for 6 minutes, stirring constantly. Pour into clean jars, filling them to overflowing, and seal tightly.

If you wish to pour this mustard into decorative mustard pots or apothecary jars, seal the hot mustard with a thin cork that is made to fit the top; when cool, cover with two thin layers of paraffin. Or use just the paraffin and cover with a cap of colored foil.

WOLFERMAN'S FAMOUS SWEET SHERRY MUSTARD
SAUCE FOR HAM OR COLD CUTS

1 cup dry mustard   3 eggs
¾ cup cider vinegar   ¾ cup sugar
¼ cup sherry

Soak mustard overnight in vinegar and sherry. Next day beat eggs and gradually beat in sugar. Add mustard-vinegar-sherry mixture and cook over simmering water until sauce is thick, stirring constantly.

Pack into screw-top jar or bottle, cover, and refrigerate. Fills an 8-ounce jar, with a little left over for a ham sandwich.

Bring a jar to a Memorial Day cookout or Labor Day picnic and you're bound to be invited back soon!

HOW TO DRY FRESH GARDEN HERBS

DRYING BUNCHES OF HERBS

Herbs should be harvested for drying just before the plants begin to flower. At this time the essential oils in the leaves are at a maximum. Cut them on a cool morning of a sunny day just after the last beads of moisture have evaporated.

The main stem of perennials should be cut about two-thirds down its length and all the side branches should be allowed to remain on the stalk. Annuals should be cut about 4 inches from the ground.

Carefully remove and discard any rusty or discolored leaves and tie leafy stems in bunches. Label each bunch carefully and hang them upside down from a cord strung in a dry, airy attic or garage. When crisply dry, take down each bunch and strip the leaves off by hand. Pack into small, tightly sealed containers and store in a dark place.

DRYING INDIVIDUAL LEAVES

Strip perfect leaves from the stalks and sprinkle them on a screen or wire mesh covered with a layer of cheesecloth. Place them in a spot where the air can circulate freely through and over the screen. Turn the leaves each day. If drying out-of-doors, bring them in every evening before the dew falls. If your drying spot is windy it may be necessary to cover the leaves lightly with cheesecloth so that they are between layers of cheesecloth to prevent them from blowing away. In good weather the leaves should be dry in about 4 days. Pack into small, tightly sealed containers and store in a dark place.

BOUQUET GARNI

These are little tied bunches or muslin bags containing a mixture of herbs used to drop into bubbling soups or stews to add tantalizing flavors.

The usual combination of "pot herbs" (also called fines herbes) are parsley, bay leaf, tarragon, and thyme, but many other combinations may be used, such as:

basil	chives	parsley	rosemary
thyme	parsley	chives	parsley
chervil	basil	tarragon	chervil
parsley	thyme	chervil	chives

POTPOURRI

There is no reason why fragrant potpourris are not as welcome a gift of love today as they were in grandmother's time. Attach one or two to your shower gift for a June bride, or give as a housewarming present.

Collect the roses in the early morning, before the sun is high, and after two or three days of dry weather. Select the freshest of flowers, ones that have not been open for more than a day or two. Remove the petals, and keep the colors separate if you wish to arrange the dried petals in a rainbowlike effect, or a combination of colors, with a whole flower such as a pansy or violet pressed against the inside of the glass container. Place petals in a thin layer on window screens or some kind of rack that will hold the petals and still let the air circulate. Window screens may be stacked one on top of the other with blocks between to separate them. Do not set the racks where the sun can strike them, and if there is too much breeze, cover the screens with cheesecloth. Leave the petals until they are very dry, stirring them gently from time to time so they will dry evenly and thoroughly. Store each color in a tight jar, away from the sun, until ready to use.

When ready to make your potpourri, put petals in a bowl and add a fixative, which may be purchased from a drugstore. (About 1 tablespoon to 1 quart of petals.) There are two kinds of fixatives—the animal fixatives, such as ambergris from whales, beavers, or civet cats; and the vegetable fixatives, such as gum benzoin, storax, or the crushed roots of calamus or orris. The vegetable fixatives are better to use as they are not so expensive and are more readily available. They should be crushed, not powdered, or they will cloud the potpourri. If the potpourri is going to be put into decorative crocks or opaque jars, there is no need to separate the colors or to worry about the colors fading.

Any number of crushed spices may be added to a potpourri in the proportion of about 1 tablespoon to a quart of potpourri. Cinnamon, nutmeg, allspice, and mace are nice. So, too, are crushed seeds of anise, caraway, coriander, cardamom, or vanilla bean. The thin peels of orange, lemon, and tangerine, cut into small pieces and each studded with a clove, are a delightful addition; the peel should be allowed to dry for 24 hours before it is added to the potpourri. A few drops of fragrant oils, which may be ordered through your local drugstore, may also be added and thoroughly mixed with the petals. Oils such as rose geranium, rosemary, lemon verbena, or peppermint are good, but be careful not to let the oil overpower the petals and don't use more than a combination of three different oils.

After the potpourri is well mixed, pack it in crocks, filling the crocks about two-thirds full and leaving enough room to let you stir the petals from time to time. Cover tightly for 6 weeks, stirring once a week and, two or three times a week, turn and rock the jar. At the end of 6 weeks, again mix thoroughly and fill decorated ceramic or glass jars. The potpourri will continue to age and improve in fragrance when repacked.

BATH HERBS

A bouquet of aromatic herbs to drop into the bath is a delightful custom, dating back over a hundred years. The herbs are supposed to relax tired muscles, relieve nervous tension, and aid poor circulation. A 3-inch square of cheesecloth is used to hold the herbs. They can be single herbs or combinations of equal parts of pennyroyal and angelica, sage and rosemary, lemon balm and peppermint; or equal parts of the flower heads of chamomile, thyme, and elder flowers. Tie the bags with colored embroidery cotton and package several together in a gift box.

OTHER UNUSUAL GIFTS THAT MAY BE MADE FROM HERBS

MOTH BAGS

More pleasant than mothballs, but just as disliked by the moths, are small muslin or cheesecloth bags holding about 1 tablespoon each of crushed dried thyme, tansy, southernwood, and crushed cloves.

Another unpopular combination for moths is dried lavender flowers, rosemary, crushed cloves, and a piece of dried lemon peel.

SACHETS

Many beautiful sachets in a variety of colors and sizes may be made from silk, velvet, or satin. Either squares or tiny bags drawn together at the top with ribbon are easy to make for anyone who is handy with the sewing machine. If you are a needlepoint addict, go ahead, needlepoint the sachets with an herb design. Fill them with a mixture of lavender, lemon verbena, sweet geranium, rose petals, and mint leaves.

CRYSTALLIZED MINT LEAVES

Wash leaves and pick them early in the morning after a warm summer rain. Let them stand on paper towels until thoroughly dry.

Combine 1 egg white with 1 tablespoon water and beat slightly. Stir in 1 drop peppermint oil. Apply the egg white with a pastry brush to each leaf, making sure each side is completely covered. Dip in fine granulated sugar, again making sure each side is well coated.

Arrange the leaves on a cake rack covered with waxed paper and dry in a very slow oven, or where there is a good current of air. Store in a snugly covered tin box; they will keep for weeks.

Crystallized mint leaves add a decorative touch to cakes or fruit cups.

HERB SUGAR

This makes a lovely sugar substitute on the tea tray. Put a handful of spearmint or peppermint leaves or a few rose geranium leaves into a glass canister and fill the jar with superfine fruit sugar. Cover and stir sugar each day for several days until the leaves are dry and the sugar is flavored with the herb. Sift out the dry leaves before using or packaging in small containers as gifts.

HERBED MINTS

2½ cups superfine fruit sugar
3 ounces cream cheese
½ teaspoon oil of peppermint

Mix and knead the sugar, cream cheese, and peppermint oil until smooth and well mixed. Roll into balls the size of marbles and flatten on waxed paper with a fork.

Keep refrigerated until ready to use. These also freeze well and may be attractively packaged in a decorative cookie tin with a tight-fitting cover.

SPICED TEAS AND TISANES

Many garden herbs may be used as a substitute for all or part of the regular tea leaves used to brew a cup of tea, and when packaged in little bags they make a thoughtful gift for tea drinkers and health addicts. Such herbs as chamomile, wild raspberry leaves, and catnip not only add a pleasing flavor but also are considered to be mildly tonic.

To make tea bags, cut a double thickness of cheesecloth into 5-inch squares. Put a teaspoon of herbs or spices or a combination of spices, fruit rinds, roots, and regular tea in the center, pull up corners to form a pouch, and tie with colorfast embroidery floss. Attach a tag on which are printed the name of the tea and instructions: "Steep this bag for 2–5 minutes in a cup of boiling water or fruit juice and serve hot or cold as a refreshing beverage." Apple, cranberry, and grape all make good fruit bases for herbed or spiced beverages.

Seed Teas: Add ½ teaspoon anise seeds, 2 or 3 whole cardamom pods, or 6 allspice to each teaspoon of regular tea in the bag.

Flower Teas: Use 1 teaspoon dried flowers of chamomile or jasmine per tea bag in place of regular tea.

Herb Teas: Use 1 teaspoon dried leaves of mint, marjoram, lemon balm, wild raspberry, catnip, bergamot, betony, burnet, costmary, or sweet woodruff in place of regular tea.

Orange Spice Tea: Use ½ teaspoon dried orange peel, ½ teaspoon anise seeds, and 2 whole allspice in each bag.

Gingered Tea: Use 1 teaspoon minced candied ginger and 1 teaspoon black tea in each bag.

3
Pickles Galore

During the many years that I lived in New York, I used to look forward to visits from my country friends and relatives who, in late summer of each year, used to load the back seat of their car with fresh vine-ripened vegetables and jar after jar of their homemade pickles, chili sauces, and relishes. Nothing they could have brought would have been more appreciated than these fragrant memories of my mother's kitchen. They were like opening the window and letting in a breath of country sunshine.

Now, living in northern New Jersey, I can make all the pickles and relishes that I want for my own table and to give to my city friends. What vegetables I cannot grow myself in sufficient quantity for preserving are inexpensively available at a nearby farmer's market. Such produce markets may be available to many city residents by nothing more than a short ride into the suburbs during the height of the vegetable season. It's well worth it, and once you have experienced the pungent aroma of various aromatic spices simmering with vinegar and sugar you'll be a pickle addict forever.

With commercial canned goods so available and comparatively cheap, it is more practical, once the freezer is bulging, to use the surplus from the garden to make the more costly savory condiments. No special equipment is needed; no cooking under pressure is necessary to kill harmful organisms that may be present in home-canned foods. Homemade pickles are a cinch to make and safe to eat. Just as sugar is the preservative in jams and jellies, vinegar and pickling salt are the preservatives in pickles, and the many different kinds of pickles make wonderful gifts from a country kitchen. There are sour pickles, sweet pickles, mustard pickles, and dills, so named for the predominating flavor; and there are ketchups, chowchows, chili sauces, relishes, and chutneys, all of which designate a type of pickle rather than a flavor. All can be changed to suit your individual taste. A mustard pickle may be made more mustardy, a garlic pickle more garlicky, a sweet pickle sweeter, and so on without fear of ruining the pickle. You may add celery seeds, allspice, ginger, cloves, turmeric, coriander, or what you choose to make a pickle particularly yours. They will all be far superior in flavor and quality than anything manufactured in quantity by commercial food processors.

Standard preserving jars may be used; so too may any other clean container providing it has a reusable screw top or a resealable lid. Label your jars attractively, tie them with a pretty ribbon, nest them in baskets partially filled with straw, and give them to your most cherished friends. You can decorate the basket, too, if you wish, or tie a bunch of fresh parsley or chives to the handle. Pickles are a natural for St. Patrick's Day (with shamrock decorations on the jar), for Father's Day, or as a humorous gift for an expecting mother.

Decorative paste-on or decal labels can sometimes be found in stationery shops, and several mail-order catalogues offer personalized labels for your kitchen products.

If you have any artistic inclinations you might enjoy studying calligraphy. Inexpensive kits are available that include pen nibs, inks, and instructions for lettering.

Undoubtedly you have your own file of "secret" family pickle recipes, but just in case you don't, I'm going to give you my choicest.

The first is an exceptionally colorful red, white, and green sour cold-pack pickle that will be sufficiently aged in time for the big holidays.

ONE WORD OF CAUTION: Be sure to use pickling salt in all recipes. This is a pure salt that does not contain any added chemicals that interfere with the brining process and can result in softening of the pickles.

SOUR COLD-PACK PICKLES

Pack clean pint jars one-quarter full with peeled, quartered onions. Add sweet red pepper, cut into squares, until jar is half full. Put in another layer of onions and sprinkle with 1 teaspoon pickling salt and 1 teaspoon mixed pickling spices. Finish by filling the jar to the top with a layer of sweet green pepper, cut into squares.

Completely fill jars with distilled white vinegar and seal. Let age for 3 months before using.

DILL PICKLES, DILL TOMATOES, OR DILL PEPPERS

Fresh grape leaves, if available
  (optional)
Large bunch fresh dill
3 tablespoons mixed pickling
  spices
1 gallon small cucumbers, green

tomatoes, or green peppers
  (or cherry tomatoes, red or
  green)
⅔ cup pickling salt
½ cup vinegar
Water

Place a layer of grape leaves and half the dill in the bottom of a gallon stone crock. Sprinkle with half the pickling spice.

Wash vegetables well and pack tightly into the crock. Cover with the remaining spice, dill, and a second layer of grape leaves. Combine salt, vinegar, and enough water to make 2 quarts. Pour over the vegetables, making sure they are well covered with the brine. Cover with cheesecloth; press the vegetables down with a heavy plate and place a weight on the plate to keep the vegetables under the brine.

Let stand at room temperature for about 2 weeks, or until fermentation ceases. Remove any scum that may accumulate from the surface every few days; wash the cloth and plate and return to the crock. Keep vegetables well covered with brine and add more fresh brine as needed, made by dissolving 1 tablespoon pickling salt in 1 pint water.

When fermentation is complete, pack the pickles into clean jars. Strain the pickle solution, heat to boiling, and fill the jars to overflowing with the hot brine. Seal and store in a cool place.

Makes about 4 quarts, or 8 pints.

DILLYBEANS

At one time, dillybeans, commercially made from a "secret" recipe, were a cocktail appetizer rage. Not long afterwards they disappeared from grocery shelves. Here's the "secret," and you'll want to make lots.

2 pounds tender "stringless" beans	2 bay leaves
2 cups water	2 small onions, peeled and thinly
2 cups white distilled vinegar	sliced
1½ teaspoons pickling salt, or to	8 hot red peppers
taste	8 cloves garlic, peeled
⅓ cup sugar	8 sprigs fresh dill

Wash beans and snip off ends. Discard any that are wilted or discolored.

In saucepan combine water, vinegar, pickling salt, sugar, bay leaves, and onions. Bring liquid to a boil and simmer for 10 minutes.

Drop beans into boiling water and cook for just 5 minutes. They must still be crisp. Drain immediately and rinse in cold water.

Pack beans upright in 8-ounce jars with a couple of slices of onion. Add 1 hot pepper, 1 clove garlic, and a sprig of dill to each jar and pour the hot vinegar mixture over the beans to overflowing. Seal immediately.

Makes 8 8-ounce jars, or 4 pints.

Thinly cut carrots and other firm vegetables may be used in place of or in addition to the beans.

COCKTAIL OKRA

2 *pounds tender fresh okra pods*
5 *pods hot red or green peppers*
5 *cloves garlic, peeled*
1 *quart distilled vinegar*

½ *cup water*
6 *tablespoons pickling salt*
1 *tablespoon celery seeds*
1 *tablespoon mustard seeds*

Wash okra and pack into clean jars with screw tops. Into each jar put 1 pepper pod and 1 clove garlic. Bring remaining ingredients to a boil and pour over the okra, filling the jars to overflowing. Seal while hot and let age for 2 months before using.

Makes 5 pints.

DILLED GREEN TOMATOES OR CHERRY TOMATOES

Select small, firm green tomatoes or cherry tomatoes. Pack the tomatoes into sterilized jars and to each quart jar add 1 clove garlic, 1 stalk celery, several strips of green pepper, and a large spray of dill. Bring to a boil 2 quarts water, 1 quart vinegar, and ½ cup pickling salt and boil for 5 minutes. Pour the hot brine over the vegetables in the jar and seal. The pickles will be ready to use in about 4 weeks.

Hot red peppers, celery seeds, and mustard seed may be added to the vinegar mixture.

SWEET PICKLED CHERRY TOMATOES

4 *pounds firm cherry tomatoes*
3½ *pounds sugar*
4 *cups water*

1 *fresh ginger root, grated*
Juice and grated rind of 2 lemons
1 *teaspoon pickling salt*

Wash the tomatoes and prick each one in several places with the tines of a fork. Dissolve the sugar in the water, bring to a boil, and boil rapidly for 5 minutes. Add the tomatoes and cook for 10 minutes. Remove the tomatoes and to the syrup add the ginger root, lemon juice and rind, and salt. Simmer the syrup for 15 minutes, return the tomatoes to the syrup, and cook for about 30 minutes longer, or until the syrup is thick and the tomatoes are transparent. Turn into hot jars and seal.

Makes about 6 pints.

These make a wonderful take-along gift if you've been invited to a picnic or a tail-gate party.

CRISP BREAD AND BUTTER PICKLES

4 quarts thinly sliced cucumbers
8 white onions, peeled and sliced
½ cup pickling salt
5 cups sugar

1½ teaspoons turmeric
1 teaspoon celery seeds
2 tablespoons mustard seed
5 cups cider vinegar

Mix the cucumbers and onions with the salt and 2 quarts cracked ice and let them stand, covered with a weighted lid, for 3 hours. Drain thoroughly and put the vegetables in a large kettle. Add the sugar, spices, and vinegar and bring almost to a boil, stirring often with a wooden spoon, but do not let boil. Pack the pickles into hot jars and seal.

Makes 7–8 pints.

Two small green peppers, seeded and sliced, may be added, and ½ teaspoon ground cloves added to the vinegar mixture give the pickles a different flavor.

ICE-WATER PICKLES

3 pounds 4-inch cucumbers
5 medium-sized onions
1 tablespoon mustard seed

1 quart cider vinegar
1 cup sugar
2 tablespoons pickling salt

Wash the cucumbers, quarter them lengthwise, and soak them in ice-water for 2 hours.

Slice the onions and pack them in the bottoms of pint jars. Pack the cucumbers lengthwise in the jars. Combine the mustard seed, vinegar, sugar, and salt, bring to a boil, and boil for 1 minute. Fill the jars to overflowing with the boiling-hot syrup and seal.

Makes 5 pints.

CURRY PICKLES

24 medium-sized cucumbers,
    thinly sliced
½ cup pickling salt
2 quarts water

1 teaspoon curry powder
2½ cups vinegar
¼ cup mustard
1 tablespoon celery seeds

Put the cucumbers in a bowl, add the salt and water, and let stand for 5 hours. Drain and rinse the cucumbers well. Combine the remaining ingredients and bring to a boil. Add the cucumbers and heat just to the boiling point. Pack into hot jars and seal.

Makes 3 pints.

PICKLED CAULIFLOWER

2 heads cauliflower
2 cups small white or silver
    skinned onions
1 cup pickling salt
1 cup sugar

3 cups white vinegar
2 tablespoons white mustard seeds
1 tablespoon celery seeds
1 small hot red pepper

Wash the cauliflowers and break them into flowerets. Scald, cool, and peel the onions. Mix the vegetables with the salt, add just enough water to cover, and let stand about 18 hours. Drain, rinse in cool water, and drain again.

Dissolve the sugar in the vinegar, add the seeds and the hot pepper, and bring to a boil. Add the vegetables and simmer for 10 minutes, or until the vegetables are barely tender. Pack the vegetables hot into hot jars, fill the jars with the boiling-hot liquid, and seal.

Makes 4 pints.

PICKLED ONIONS

1 gallon pickling onions
1 cup pickling salt
1–2 cups sugar
5 cups white vinegar
3 tablespoons white mustard seeds

2 tablespoons horseradish or
    peppercorns
Hot red peppers
Bay leaves

Scald the onions for 2 minutes in boiling water, dip into cold water, and peel. Sprinkle the onions with the salt, add cold water to cover, and let stand for 12 hours, or overnight. In the morning, drain the onions, rinse them in cold, fresh water, and drain again.

Combine the sugar, vinegar, mustard seeds, and horseradish or peppercorns, bring to a boil, and simmer for 15 minutes. Pack the onions into clean jars. Add 1 small hot pepper and 1 bay leaf to each jar, fill the jars with the boiling-hot liquid, and seal.

Makes 5–6 pints.

Add 6 tablespoons whole allspice or ¼ cup mixed pickling spices for interesting variations.

FAVORITE MUSTARD PICKLES

12 *medium-sized cucumbers*

6 *medium-sized onions, peeled*

6 *red peppers, seeded*

2 *quarts gherkins*

2 *quarts small white or silver*
   skinned onions, peeled

2 *heads cauliflower, broken into*
   bite-sized flowerets

1½ *cups pickling salt*

8 *cups sugar*

8 *cups cider vinegar*

1½ *cups flour*

½ *cup dry mustard*

3 *tablespoons turmeric*

2 *tablespoons celery salt*

Finely chop or grind through the medium blade of a food chopper the cucumbers, onions, and red pepper, and put each ground vegetable in a separate bowl. Also put into separate bowls the gherkins, white onions, and the cauliflower flowerets. Sprinkle each vegetable with the salt, using about ¼ cup to each bowl. Cover the gherkins, pickling onions, and cauliflower with cold water and let all the vegetables stand overnight. In the morning, drain the chopped vegetables in a colander; drain the whole vegetables and dry them on a towel. Mix the vegetables in a preserving kettle, stir in the sugar and 6 cups of the vinegar, and bring the mixture to a boil.

Combine the flour, mustard, turmeric, and celery salt and mix them to a smooth paste with the remaining vinegar. Stir the paste gradually into the vegetables and continue to stir until the sauce is slightly thickened. Turn the pickles into jars and seal at once.

Makes 6 quarts.

AUNT MAY'S PICKLED GREEN TOMATOES

2 *gallons sliced fresh green*
   tomatoes (about 15 pounds)

1 *cup pickling salt*

½ *tablespoon powdered alum*

2 *quarts boiling water*

2 *cups cider vinegar*

5 *cups sugar*

2 *sticks cinnamon*

Handful cloves

Arrange the tomatoes in layers in a large bowl or pickle crock, sprinkling the salt between the layers. Let stand overnight. The next day, drain, sprinkle with the alum, and pour the boiling water over them. Let stand for 20 minutes. Drain, rinse, and drain again.

In an enamel or stainless steel preserving kettle combine cider vinegar, sugar, and the spices, tied in a cheesecloth bag. (The spice bag should be kept in the syrup right up to the very end.) Bring to a boil, stirring until sugar is dissolved, and boil rapidly for 3 minutes. Pour the syrup over the tomatoes and let stand overnight.

Next day, drain off syrup and bring to a boil. Pour over tomatoes and let stand again overnight.

On the fourth day, put syrup and tomatoes into the kettle, bring to a boil, and simmer until the tomatoes are transparent.

Pack the tomatoes into hot jars. Boil the syrup until it becomes quite thick, or spins a long thread. Remove the spice bag and pour the syrup over the fruit, filling the jars, and seal.

Makes 8 quarts.

CRISP PICKLED WATERMELON RIND

Peel and remove all the green and pink portions from the rind of a large watermelon. Cut the rind into cubes or slices and measure 4 quarts. Drop the rind into a kettle of boiling water, boil for 5 minutes, and drain. Cool.

Dissolve 4 tablespoons slaked lime (obtainable at your drugstore) in 2 quarts cold water. Pour the solution over the watermelon rind and let stand for 3 hours. Drain and rinse thoroughly.

Cover the rind with clear cold water, bring to a boil, and boil until the rind is tender. Drain.

Combine 2 cups sugar, 1 cup vinegar, and 4 cups water. Add 2 tablespoons each of whole allspice and whole cloves, 4 sticks cinnamon, and 2 pieces ginger root, all tied in a bag. Bring to a boil and boil for 5 minutes. Add the rind and 2 hot peppers, bring again to a boil, and simmer for 30 minutes. Let the rind stand in the syrup in a cool place for 12–24 hours. Add 3 cups vinegar and 2–4 cups sugar according to taste, bring to a boil, and simmer until the rind is transparent. If the syrup becomes too thick before the rind is clear, add ½ cup hot water from time to time as needed. Discard the spice bag, pack the rind and the boiling-hot syrup into hot jars, and seal.

Makes 8 pints.

GREEN TOMATO RELISH

6 pounds green tomatoes	1½ cups vinegar
3 medium-sized onions	2 teaspoons white peppercorns
4 tablespoons pickling salt	2 teaspoons whole allspice
5 thin slices lemon	2 teaspoons whole cloves
¾ cup finely chopped fresh sweet red pepper	2 teaspoons celery seeds
1½ cups brown sugar	2 teaspoons mustard seeds
	2 teaspoons dry mustard

Wash and core the tomatoes; peel the onions. Slice the tomatoes and onions thinly, mix with the salt, and let stand overnight. In the morning, drain thoroughly. Put the tomatoes and onions in a large kettle and add the lemon slices, pepper, sugar, vinegar, and the spices and mustard, tied in a bag. Bring to a boil and cook for about 30 minutes, or until slightly thickened, stirring occasionally. Discard the spice bag and turn the relish into hot jars. Seal at once.

Makes 4 quarts.

JERUSALEM ARTICHOKE OR "SUN CHOKE" RELISH

3 tablespoons pickling salt
1 quart peeled, coarsely ground
    Jerusalem artichokes
4 cups minced or ground onion
2 cups ground fresh sweet red
    pepper
1 quart distilled vinegar

2 cups sugar
1 teaspoon celery seeds
½ teaspoon cayenne
2 tablespoons mustard seeds
1 tablespoon turmeric
2 tablespoons dry mustard

Sprinkle salt over the ground artichokes and let stand for 1 hour. Squeeze the chokes, discarding the liquid that has accumulated. In a heavy kettle combine artichokes, onion, pepper, vinegar, sugar, celery seeds, cayenne, mustard seeds, turmeric, and dry mustard. Stir well, bring to a boil, and boil rapidly for 10 minutes. Pour while hot into clean jars and seal immediately.

Makes 4–5 pints.

Any firm vegetable may be substituted for the Jerusalem artichokes.

HOT DOG RELISH

3 pounds sweet red peppers,
    seeded
3 pounds sweet green peppers,
    seeded
3 pounds onions, peeled
4 cups cider vinegar

½ cup sugar
1 teaspoon mustard seeds
1 teaspoon dry mustard
1 teaspoon celery seeds
2 tablespoons salt

Put the vegetables through the medium blade of a food chopper. Cover the vegetables with boiling water, let stand for 15 minutes, and drain well. Add the remaining ingredients, bring to a boil, and cook for 10 minutes, stirring occasionally. Turn into hot jars and seal.

Makes 8 pints.

This would make a nice "thank-you" gift to the den or troop mother who's volunteered to hold the annual cook-out.

INDIA RELISH

12 *medium-sized cucumbers*	1 *cup water*
6 *green tomatoes*	4 *tablespoons sugar*
2 *ripe tomatoes*	1 *teaspoon ground cinnamon*
2 *sweet green peppers*	1 *teaspoon turmeric*
2 *sweet red peppers*	1/4 *teaspoon ground cloves*
2 *onions*	1/2 *teaspoon ground allspice*
1/4 *cup pickling salt*	2 *tablespoons white mustard seeds*
4 *cups vinegar*	

Slice the cucumbers and green tomatoes; peel and slice the ripe tomatoes. Seed and chop the peppers; peel and finely chop the onions. Mix the vegetables with the salt and let stand overnight.

Drain the vegetables, add 2 cups of the vinegar and the water, and bring slowly to a boil. Drain again. Mix the sugar, cinnamon, turmeric, cloves, and allspice to a smooth paste with a little of the vinegar. Bring the remaining vinegar to a boil, stir in the paste, and add the white mustard seeds and the vegetables. Bring to a boil and cook for 20 minutes, stirring constantly. Turn into hot jars and seal.

Makes 8 pints.

SPICY CORN RELISH

2 *cups chopped fresh sweet red*	2 *tablespoons pickling salt*
pepper	2 *teaspoons powdered celery seeds*
2 *cups chopped fresh sweet green*	2 *tablespoons dry mustard*
pepper	1/4 *cup flour*
2 *cups chopped celery*	1 *tablespoon turmeric*
1 *cup chopped onion*	1/2 *cup water*
1 *cup sugar*	2 *quarts cooked cut corn*
1 *quart cider vinegar*	

Into a large preserving kettle put the pepper, celery, onion, sugar, vinegar, salt, and celery seed. Bring to a boil and boil for 15 minutes, stirring occasionally. Combine the mustard, flour, and turmeric and stir in the water to make a smooth paste. Stir the paste gradually into the relish, add the corn, and bring again to a boil. Boil for 5 minutes, stirring constantly. Seal hot in hot jars.

Makes 6 pints.

Two cups shredded cabbage may be substituted for the sweet green pepper, if desired.

PICCALILLI

1 *quart chopped green tomatoes*	½ *cup salt*
2 *red peppers, seeded and chopped*	3 *cups cider vinegar*
2 *green peppers, seeded and*	2 *cups brown sugar*
chopped	1 *3-inch stick cinnamon*
2 *large onions, peeled and chopped*	1 *teaspoon cloves*
1 *small head cabbage, shredded, or*	1 *teaspoon allspice*
2 *cups chopped cucumber*	1 *teaspoon mustard seeds*

Combine all the vegetables and the salt and let stand overnight. In the morning, drain the vegetables, pressing out the juice. Add the vinegar, sugar, and the spices, tied in a bag; bring to a boil and simmer until the vegetables are clear and the syrup is thickened. Discard the spice bag and seal the piccalilli in hot jars.

Makes 8 pints.

One tablespoon each peppercorns and celery seeds may be substituted for the cinnamon.

SWEET PEPPER RELISH

12 *sweet green peppers, seeded*	4 *cups cider vinegar*
12 *sweet red peppers, seeded*	2 *cups sugar*
12 *medium-sized onions, peeled*	2 *tablespoons pickling salt*

Cut peppers into strips and quarter the onions. Put vegetables through the coarse blade of a food grinder or chop in a food processor. Put vegetables into a heavy kettle and pour boiling water over them to cover. Let stand 10 minutes, then drain. Add the vinegar, sugar, and salt to the vegetables. Mix well. Bring to a boil and simmer for 20 minutes. Pour into clean jars while hot and seal.

Makes 10 pints.

TACO SAUCE

6–8 *fresh ripe tomatoes, peeled*   1 *tablespoon cayenne*
    and coarsely cut   2 *cloves garlic, peeled*
1 *tablespoon ground cumin*   ½ *teaspoon pickling salt*
1 *teaspoon crumbled oregano*

Blend all ingredients in container of a blender on low speed for 10 seconds, then pour into saucepan and bring to a boil. Remove from heat immediately. Cool and pour into bottles. Seal and store in refrigerator.

    Makes about 1 quart.

RED-HOT PEPPER SAUCE

24 *long hot peppers*   1 *tablespoon pickling salt*
12 *ripe tomatoes*   2 *tablespoons mixed pickling*
4 *cups vinegar*   *spices*
1 *cup sugar*

Wash and drain the vegetables. Seed and chop the peppers; core and chop the tomatoes. Put the vegetables in a kettle with 2 cups of the vinegar, bring to a boil, and boil until vegetables are soft. Press the mixture through a fine sieve. Add the sugar and salt and the spices, tied in a bag, and boil until the sauce is thick. Add the remaining vinegar and continue to boil for about 15 minutes, or until the sauce is the desired consistency. Discard the spice bag and seal, boiling-hot, in hot jars.

    Makes about 8 pints.

FAVORITE CHILI SAUCE

25 *large ripe tomatoes*   2 *cups cider vinegar*
3 *sweet red peppers, seeded and*   1½ *cups light brown sugar*
    chopped   2 *tablespoons pickling salt*
1 *small bunch celery, chopped*   1 *teaspoon pepper*
6 *onions, chopped*   1 *teaspoon dry mustard*
3 *cloves garlic, minced*
2 *tablespoons whole allspice, tied*
    in a bag

Scald, peel, core, and quarter the tomatoes. Squeeze out the seeds and excess juice and finely chop the pulp. Put the pulp in a large kettle, bring to a boil, and boil rapidly until the tomatoes are soft. Ladle off the clear liquid that comes to the top of the tomatoes while they are cooking. Add the remaining ingredients and cook for 30 minutes. Discard the spice bag and continue to cook for about 1 hour longer, or until thick, stirring occasionally. Seal in hot sterilized jars.

Makes 4–6 pints.

TOMATO KETCHUP

16 pounds ripe tomatoes	*2 teaspoons dry mustard*
3 sweet red peppers, seeded	*1 teaspoon paprika*
2 onions, peeled	*1 tablespoon whole allspice*
2 tablespoons pickling salt	*1 tablespoon whole cloves*
½ cup sugar	*1 tablespoon broken cinnamon*
2 teaspoons celery salt	*2 cups cider vinegar*

Chop the tomatoes, peppers, and onions, put them in a kettle, and cook until soft. Press the mixture through a fine sieve and measure the purée. There should be 4 quarts purée. To the purée add the salt, sugar, celery salt, mustard, and paprika, and the whole spices, tied in a bag. Bring to a boil and cook rapidly for 1 hour. Discard the spice bag. Add the vinegar and continue to cook until the ketchup is thick. Seal in hot sterilized jars or bottles.

Makes 6 pints.

For a really hot ketchup, add 2 teaspoons ground black pepper and ½ teaspoon cayenne.

CURRY POWDER

¼ cup poppy seeds	*1 teaspoon cardamom*
¼ cup coriander	*1 teaspoon peppercorns*
2 tablespoons ground turmeric	*1 teaspoon ground ginger*
1 tablespoon cumin seed	*4 bay leaves*
1 4–6-inch stick cinnamon	*12 small hot chili peppers*
10 whole cloves	

Place all ingredients in a shallow baking pan. Bake in 200° oven for 25 minutes, stirring occasionally. Blend ingredients on high speed in a blender for 60 seconds, or until pulverized.

Makes 1 cup.

For gift-giving, package your unique bright orange curry in a charming apothecary jar and pack a jar in a basket with a container of your homemade chutney, a can of peanuts, and a tiny bottle of saffron threads if you wish. And your own favorite recipe for curry. Tie it all together with a bright bow.

INDIAN CHUTNEY

2 apples, cored, pared, and
    chopped (2 cups)
½ cup chopped onion
½ cup seedless raisins
⅓ cup vinegar
¼ cup brown sugar
¼ cup water

2 tablespoons candied citron
1 tablespoon curry powder
½ teaspoon salt
½ teaspoon ground ginger
⅛ teaspoon ground cloves
⅛ teaspoon ground cinnamon
2 cloves garlic, minced

In a saucepan combine all ingredients. Cook, uncovered, over low heat for 45–60 minutes, stirring occasionally to prevent sticking. Chill.

    Makes 1⅓ cups.

APPLE CHUTNEY

1 quart cider vinegar
3 cups sugar
½ pound seedless raisins
6 pounds sour apples, peeled,
    quartered, and cored
¼ pound garlic, peeled and
    chopped
½ pound green ginger, peeled
    and chopped

6 red or green chili peppers,
    seeded and chopped
2 tablespoons pickling salt
Sugar to taste
Cayenne to taste
6 pounds hard green pears,
    peeled, cored, and cut into
    strips

In large preserving kettle mix the vinegar, sugar, raisins, apples, garlic, ginger, peppers, and salt. Bring to a boil and simmer until the apples are mushy and transparent. If necessary, add a little more vinegar. Taste and add sugar and cayenne as desired. Then add the pears and simmer until the pears are transparent but not overcooked.

    Makes 8–10 pints.

4

Hostess Gifts that Money Can't Buy

Seldom does anyone go out to dinner or to a friend's home for the weekend without taking along a gift that says "thank you." It need not be expensive, SHOULD not be, as a matter of fact, for a costly gift could be a source of embarrassment to your hostess. It should be just a token of your appreciation.

A bottle of fine wine, a wedge of excellent aged cheese, purchased en route to your destination, are considered perfectly okay hostess gifts. Far better, of course, are those gifts with a personal touch, something you have made in your own kitchen, gifts that money can't buy, gifts that express so eloquently—"I care."

Whether you decide to take along a sumptuous liver pâté in an earthenware crock, a ceramic ginger jar filled with toasted almonds, a pretty wicker basket lined with a colorful kitchen towel topped with some sweet rolls, or some particularly useful kitchen gadget to which you have tied one of your favorite recipes and boxed with a gay pot holder, will depend on how far you have to go and whether you are walking a few blocks, taking a bus to the other end of town, driving for several hours into city or countryside, or taxiing to an airport to catch a plane. Certainly you would not want to take a product that is spillable, leakable, or breakable on a long trip, or something that might melt or spoil while driving in a car on a hot summer's day. Common sense should be the determining factor in selecting the right hostess gift to suit your convenience and the occasion.

When joining nearby friends for a casual cocktail hour, take along a favorite appetizer and you'll be sure to be invited back soon! Should it be the host or hostess's birthday or some other special occasion, pack one or more of your homemade canapé spreads or butters in French butter dishes, china ramekins, or crocks, then set them on a tray or in a basket, tuck in a spreading knife (anything from sterling to plastic), and surround with some tiny baking powder or benne biscuits.

PÂTÉS FOR GIFT-GIVING

Chicken liver pâtés are among the most popular canapé spreads, and there are dozens of different recipes, from the very simple to the more complex. Try several to find your favorite, then add your own touch to make it your special pâté. They keep for at least a week in the refrigerator and take kindly to freezing.

The first is a cinch to make.

CHICAGO CHICKEN LIVER PÂTÉ

2 pounds chicken livers, chopped
3 sticks butter, at room
   temperature
2 medium-sized onions, chopped
1 teaspoon paprika

1 teaspoon curry powder
¼ teaspoon salt
¼ teaspoon black pepper
¼ cup cognac

In a large saucepan combine the livers, 1 stick butter, the onions, paprika, curry powder, salt, and pepper. Cook over moderate heat for about 10 minutes, stirring frequently. Empty into container of an electric blender and blend on high speed until pâté is smooth, stopping to stir down occasionally. Empty into a bowl and beat in the remaining butter, bit by bit, and finally the cognac. Pack in a bowl or crock with a cover and chill until firm or freeze in the container.

Makes 8–10 servings.

PÂTÉ MAISON

"Pâté Maison" means the special pâté of the house or restaurant. Some are coarse country pâtés; others are smooth and unctuous like this one.

3 shallots, minced
2 tablespoons minced parsley
½ cup butter (1 stick)
1 pound chicken livers, cleaned
   and halved
1 pound calf's liver, cubed

1 cup melted sweet butter or
   rendered chicken fat
4 tablespoons brandy
4 egg yolks
¼ cup heavy cream
¼ teaspoon dry thyme
Salt and white pepper to taste

In saucepan cook the shallots and parsley in the ½ cup butter until shallots are tender but not brown. Add chicken livers and calf's liver and cook over low heat for about 15 minutes, stirring occasionally. Empty half the liver into container of an electric blender, add half the melted butter and half the brandy, and blend on high speed until smooth. Empty into a mixing bowl and repeat with remaining livers, butter, and brandy.

Beat the egg yolks and cream and stir into the liver mixture with the thyme, salt, and pepper.

Empty mixture into a 6-cup casserole or a 9 x 5-inch loaf pan, cover with lid of casserole or with foil, and bake at 300° for 1½ hours. Cool and chill. May be frozen in the casserole.

Makes 6 cups.

Serve cold with thinly sliced pumpernickel. For gift-giving, include a crusty loaf of your own French bread.

CHICKEN LIVER PÂTÉ WITH WINE

½ pound chicken livers
½ pound sweet butter
½ cup chopped shallots or spring
*   onion*
¼ cup Madeira or Marsala

Salt and freshly ground black
*   pepper to taste*
¼ teaspoon nutmeg
Clarified butter (see page 59)

Clean the chicken livers, discarding the connecting tissue, and cut in half.

In heavy skillet heat the butter and in it sauté the chicken livers for about 6 minutes, or until just cooked through. Lift out livers with a slotted spoon and set aside.

In butter remaining in skillet sauté shallots or onion until transparent but not brown. Add the wine and bring to a simmer, stirring in all the nice brown bits from bottom and sides of skillet.

Pour contents of skillet into container of an electric blender, add chicken livers, and blend on high speed until livers and shallots are reduced to a smooth paste. Spoon out into a bowl and season with salt, pepper, and nutmeg. Mix well and pack into small terrines, casseroles, or crocks. Seal with a ⅛-inch layer of clarified butter.

Makes 2 cups.

DEAN'S MOCK FOIE GRAS

This is my favorite pâté and one that comes the closest to the expensive imported foie gras, or goose liver pâté. An added dividend is that it is easy to make.

1 pound chicken livers, cleaned
   and halved
¾ pound butter
3 small onions, finely chopped
4 cloves garlic, minced

1 bay leaf
Pinch each of dried oregano, sweet
   basil, thyme
2 tablespoons Marsala or brandy

Put all ingredients but the Marsala or brandy into a casserole with a tight-fitting lid. Bake in a 350° oven for 1 hour. Empty into blender container, add the Marsala or brandy, and blend on high speed, stopping to stir down if necessary, until smooth. Pack into small bowls or ramekins and chill. This may be unmolded if desired and surrounded by sliced dark bread or crackers.

Makes about 1 quart.

To keep for any length of time in refrigerator, cover tops of containers with ⅛-inch layer of clarified butter or rendered chicken fat (see below) to seal out the air. Freeze if desired.

COARSE LIVER PÂTÉ

½ pound fresh larding pork, cut
   into thin slices
1½ pounds chicken livers
½ cup coarsely chopped pistachio
   nuts
¾ pound ground veal
¾ pound ground pork
½ cup Madeira or port

2 eggs
1½ teaspoons salt
½ teaspoon ground allspice
½ teaspoon coarsely ground
   pepper
1 teaspoon ginger
½ teaspoon thyme

Line a 9 x 5 x 3-inch loaf pan with thin slices of larding pork, reserving some for the top of the pâté.

Dice the chicken livers and combine with remaining ingredients, mixing well. Spoon into prepared pan and pack down well with back of the spoon. Cover the top with larding pork, then with aluminum foil. Bake in a 375° oven for 3 hours.

Remove pâté from oven and place a heavy weight directly on the pâté in the pan. Cool, then refrigerate. It will keep for at least ten days in refrigerator or may be frozen.

Makes 8–10 servings.

CLARIFIED BUTTER

Put a couple of sticks of butter into a heavy saucepan. Melt butter over low heat and continue to cook until there is a light brown sediment in the bottom of the pan. The butter must remain golden. When butter is clear, remove saucepan from the heat, skim off any foam from the top, and let the butter cool. Then pour it carefully into a crock or bowl, being careful not to include any of the sediment from the bottom. It will keep almost indefinitely in the refrigerator.

RENDERED CHICKEN FAT

Cut chicken fat into small pieces and put them in a saucepan over low heat. Heat the fat until bits of it become gray-looking rather than yellow. Then add 1 small onion, minced, for each pound of chicken fat and continue to cook over low heat until both the onion and bits of fat are brown. Strain into a clean jar, cover, and refrigerate. It will keep indefinitely in the refrigerator.

The little bits of brown chicken skin that remain after the chicken fat has been rendered are a crisp addition to a chicken liver pâté.

JEWISH-STYLE CHOPPED CHICKEN LIVERS

1 pound chicken fat
3 Spanish onions, finely chopped
1 pound chicken livers, cleaned and halved
4 hard-cooked eggs
Salt and coarsely ground black pepper

Render the chicken fat (see above). Put onions into a skillet and place over medium heat. Cover skillet tightly and let the onions braise in their own juice until transparent and tender. Add ⅔ cup of the rendered chicken fat and sauté the onions in it until golden. Remove onions with a slotted spoon and in fat remaining in skillet sauté the chicken livers until no blood comes out when pricked deeply with a fork. Sprinkle livers with a little salt and pepper.

Grind onions, livers, and eggs in a meat grinder or with the cutting blade in a food processor, adding any pan drippings to the mixture. Then mix well with a spoon and correct the seasoning with salt and pepper. Add 4 tablespoons rendered chicken fat and pack into a 1-quart terrine. Cover the top of the livers with a little chicken fat and refrigerate. It will keep for more than a week.

Makes 1 quart.

CHEESES FOR GIFT-GIVING

Potted cheese, or a cheese ball or spread, alone or with homemade bread or crackers, on a small wooden or plastic tray, make fine carry-in-hand gifts to take to your hostess for a dinner invitation, bridge club meeting, or after-theater party.

POTTED CHEESE

1 pound soft cheese (all one kind or a combination of cheddar, Swiss, Liederkranz, blue, or whatever pleases your palate), shredded	2 sticks butter, at room temperature ¼ cup cognac, sherry, or beer 2 tablespoons Worcestershire sauce Cayenne or red pepper

In bowl of an electric mixer beat the cheese. Add butter and beat until mixture is light and fluffy. Beat in remaining ingredients, seasoning quite highly with cayenne or red pepper.

Pack into small decorative containers and freeze until needed.

Makes 3 cups.

SMOKY CHEESE BALL

8 ounces cream cheese	½ cup chopped parsley
4 ounces blue cheese	1 clove garlic, minced
1 5-ounce jar sharp cheddar cheese spread	1 tablespoon Worcestershire sauce ½ teaspoon hot pepper sauce
1 6-ounce roll smoked cheese	1 cup finely chopped pecans

In an electric mixer beat together all ingredients except half the pecans. When well blended, shape into a ball and roll the ball in the chopped pecans, coating it thoroughly. Wrap in foil and keep cold until ready to serve.

Makes 1½-pound ball.

LIPTOI CHEESE SPREAD

½ pound cream cheese	1 tablespoon paprika
¼ cup sour cream	2 teaspoons caraway seeds
¼ cup soft butter	2 tablespoons dry vermouth
1 tablespoon chopped capers	½ teaspoon dry mustard
1 tablespoon chopped chives or green onion tops	

Blend half the ingredients at a time in container of an electric blender. Blend until smooth, stopping to stir down occasionally. Pack into small crocks and serve chilled with thinly sliced pumpernickel.

Makes 4 4-ounce containers.

This spread does not freeze well.

PIMIENTO OLIVE CHEESE SPREAD

½ pound blue cheese
½ pound cream cheese
1 cup butter
1 cup chopped pimiento-stuffed
*   green olives*

1 tablespoon each chopped chives
*   and parsley*
1 clove garlic, minced
3 tablespoons Madeira, port, or
*   brandy*
¾ cup roasted sesame seeds

Cream together blue cheese, cream cheese, and butter. Beat in olives, chives, and parsley. Blend in garlic and Madeira, port, or brandy.

Pack mixture into small crocks and sprinkle lavishly with sesame seeds. Freeze if desired.

Makes 3 8-ounce containers.

CURRIED CHEESE PÂTÉ

6 ounces cream cheese, softened
1 cup shredded sharp cheddar
*   cheese*
1 tablespoon dry sherry

½ teaspoon curry powder
Salt to taste
1 8-ounce jar mango chutney,
*   finely chopped*
Chopped chives

Beat together until thoroughly combined the cream cheese, cheddar, sherry, curry powder, and salt. Stir in chutney.

Pack into 3 or 4 6-ounce ramekins or custard cups and sprinkle tops lavishly with chopped chives. Cover with foil and refrigerate or freeze.

For gift-giving, put the dish in the center of a small wooden cheese board and surround with sesame seed wafers or benne biscuits.

PECAN CHEESE SPREAD

⅓ cup blue cheese, at room
*   temperature*
⅓ cup shredded sharp cheddar
*   cheese, at room temperature*
3 ounces cream cheese, at room
*   temperature*

1½ tablespoons sherry
2 tablespoons minced onion or
*   chives*
½ cup finely chopped pecans
Chopped parsley

Mix all ingredients, except parsley. Garnish with parsley and serve with crackers.

Makes 1¼ cups.

POTTED CHEESE WITH PISTACHIO NUTS

½ pound shredded Swiss cheese   *½ cup cubed Swiss cheese*
1 stick soft butter   *½ cup chopped pistachio nuts*
Cream

Mash the Swiss cheese with butter, adding as much cream as needed to make a rather soft spread. Fold in the cubed cheese and pistachio nuts and pack into a bowl or small decorative crocks. Wrap and refrigerate or freeze.

Makes 2½–3 cups.

Recipe may be doubled.

ALL-AMERICAN CHEESE SPREAD

Mash 4 ounces Liederkranz cheese with 2 tablespoons soft butter. Season to taste with freshly ground black pepper and stir in 1 tablespoon chopped chives or green onion tops.

Pack into a 6-ounce ramekin or custard cup.

This is an exceptionally delicious spread for thin slices of rye or pumpernickel bread.

SESAME CHEESE SPREAD

½ pound blue cheese   *1 tablespoon chopped chives*
½ pound cream cheese   *1 tablespoon chopped parsley*
2 sticks butter, at room   *½ teaspoon garlic salt*
* temperature*   *3 tablespoons cognac*
1 cup chopped pimiento-stuffed   *¾ cup roasted sesame seeds*
* green olives*

Cream together the blue cheese, cream cheese, and butter. Add all remaining ingredients except sesame seeds and mix thoroughly. Pack into a quart crock or bowl and sprinkle top lavishly with sesame seeds, or pack into a round ball and coat with the seeds.

If mixture is too soft to form into a ball, chill for a while in refrigerator. It will keep in the refrigerator for weeks if well covered.

Makes about 5 cups.

HERBED CHEESE

1 pound cream cheese or
    Camembert, or ½ pound of
    each
½ stick butter, at room
    temperature

2 tablespoons each minced chives
    and parsley
2 tablespoons chopped capers
1 tablespoon caraway seeds
Salt and pepper to taste

Mix and mash all ingredients together, adding a little salt and pepper if needed.

Pack into small containers and cover with foil tops or lids. Store in refrigerator and serve with thinly sliced pumpernickel or crackers.

Makes about 1½ pounds.

POTTED FISH, HAM, SHRIMP, AND PORK

The following recipes make very elegant gifts; package them in small soufflé dishes of fine china and give for Thanksgiving, or take one along when the boss gives a cocktail party.

POTTED FISH

1 cup firmly packed flaked cooked
    halibut or salmon
2 sticks sweet butter, at room
    temperature
Salt and freshly ground white
    pepper

½ teaspoon nutmeg
Cayenne to taste
1 teaspoon herb vinegar (tarragon,
    dill, or basil)
Clarified butter (see page 59)

Mash together the fish and butter and season to taste with salt and pepper. Stir in remaining ingredients and pack into small pots, ramekins, or custard cups. Seal with a ⅛-inch layer of clarified butter. Freezes well.

Makes about 2 cups.

POTTED HAM

1 pound cooked smoked ham
½ pound sweet butter, at room
    temperature
Salt and freshly ground black
    pepper to taste

½ teaspoon ground mace
¼ cup port or Madeira
Clarified butter (see page 59)

Put the ham through the fine blade of a meat grinder or chop finely in a food processor. Gradually add the butter, mashing all together until mixture is well blended. If necessary add a little salt and some freshly ground pepper and stir in the mace and wine.

Pack into small pots or jars and cover with a layer of clarified butter. The layer of butter should be at least ⅛ inch thick, or thick enough to seal out the air. Store in refrigerator. May be frozen.

Makes about 3 cups.

POTTED SHRIMP

1 pound tiny Icelandic shrimp, defrosted or canned
1½ sticks butter
¼ teaspoon freshly grated nutmeg
Sprinkling of cayenne
Salt to taste

Dry the shrimp well. In a saucepan melt 1 stick of the butter with the nutmeg and cayenne. Add the shrimp and toss over very low heat until shrimp are well coated with the spiced butter. Add salt to taste and spoon the shrimp into a small container.

Melt remaining butter over low heat. Pour a layer of the warm, clarified butter over the surface of the shrimp and chill until the butter is set. If the butter layer is left untouched, shrimp will keep in the refrigerator for two weeks, or in the freezer for several months.

Makes about 3 cups.

Serve on thinly sliced rye or whole wheat bread as an appetizer.

As variations, use curry in addition to or in place of the nutmeg. Or use 2 tablespoons chopped fresh dill in place of the nutmeg.

RILLETTES OR POTTED PORK

1 pound lean pork shoulder, cut into 1-inch pieces
1 pound salt pork, cut into 1-inch squares
½ teaspoon freshly ground black pepper
½ teaspoon thyme
1 bay leaf
Salt

Put the pork into a heavy casserole with a tight-fitting lid. Rinse the pork fat in cold running water to remove the surface salt and add to the pork. Add enough water to cover and bring to a boil. Add the pepper, thyme, and bay leaf. Cover and cook in a 250° oven for 4 hours, checking occasionally to be sure it is only simmering and that there is sufficient liquid in the casserole to keep the meat moist. If there isn't, add a little boiling water.

Remove from oven to cool a little. Then discard bay leaf and strain the meat, reserving the drained-off fat and liquid. Put about half the pork into the container of an electric blender and add ½ cup of the reserved fat mixture. Cover and blend to a coarse spread, adding a little more of the liquid if necessary. Remove to a mixing bowl and repeat with the other half of the pork and another ½ cup of the reserved fat. Correct seasoning, adding a little salt if necessary.

Pack the pork into 6-ounce jars, leaving ½ inch at the top of each jar. Fill the jars with the remaining reserved liquid.

Makes 4 6-ounce jars.

For gift-giving, pack a jar of this, with one or two other small containers of unusual homemade appetizers, on a wooden tray with a small spreading knife and a loaf of homemade bread or a package of melba toast.

HOME-TOASTED NUTS

Home-toasted nuts, plain or flavored, make excellent hostess gifts and travel well if packaged in light cardboard boxes or small cookie tins lined with aluminum foil. Small ceramic ginger jars may also be used and will arrive intact if the cover is tightly secured with a ribbon and the jar is carefully packaged in a box filled with shredded paper or styrofoam balls.

ALMONDS OR HAZELNUTS TOASTED IN BUTTER

The nuts must first be blanched. To do this, crack the shells if nuts are whole and remove the nuts. Cover the nuts with boiling water and let stand for 1 minute. Drain and rinse the nuts in cool water. Slip off the skins.

Now the nuts must be dried. Spread them on a rimmed baking sheet and bake in a 350° oven for 15 minutes, shaking the pan frequently.

[Now they are ready to be used whole, halved, or chopped.]

In a small skillet heat 2 tablespoons butter and add 1 cup blanched, dried almonds or hazelnuts. Cook, stirring constantly, until nuts are lightly browned. Remove from heat and continue to stir; the nuts will continue to brown from the heat of the pan. Empty onto paper towels and sprinkle with coarse salt.

SPICED CANDIED WALNUTS

In a heavy saucepan combine ½ teaspoon each ground nutmeg, cinnamon, and allspice, ¼ teaspoon salt, 2 cups sugar, and ½ cup water. Bring slowly to a boil, then boil rapidly until the syrup spins a fine thread when a few drops are allowed to run off the tines of a fork. Remove syrup from heat and stir in 2 cups walnut halves and 2 teaspoons vanilla. Beat until syrup becomes opaque. Empty out onto a well-buttered shallow pan or plate to cool. When cool, separate nuts and store in airtight containers.

"OUCH" NUTS

4 tablespoons crushed red pepper
4 tablespoons olive oil
4 cloves garlic, lightly bruised
1½ pounds cocktail peanuts
Coarse salt if needed

In a large heavy skillet heat red pepper in the olive oil for 1 minute. Add the garlic and peanuts and cook over moderate heat for 5 minutes, stirring constantly. Drain on paper towels. If necessary, sprinkle nuts with a little coarse salt.

FROM ONE GOOD COOK TO ANOTHER

Often the distance between you and your friends or relatives with whom you would like to share your ideas from your kitchen is too far to make it practical to send the actual home-prepared food itself. You can compromise with many imaginative culinary gifts that would be just as appreciated as the actual product.

If you happen to have some "kooky" cooking friends as I have, gift-giving becomes a battle of wits to see who can come up with the most original and often amusing combination of kitchen gadgets with instructions for their use.

A few of the more obvious cook's gifts might be:

A file box attractively decorated with paper, felt, or decals, containing index cards and some of your favorite recipes, hand-written on file cards.

A pretty copper mold holding a can of toasted almonds and an attached recipe for almond pudding.

A cheese grater with a well-wrapped wedge of aged cheese and a recipe for cheese fondue.

A flexible rubber spatula, a bag of your own mixed dried herbs, and a recipe for omelet fines herbes tied to the handle of a small omelet pan containing a colorful pot holder.

A container of water-ground cornmeal, some assorted wooden spoons, and a recipe for crisp corn bread.

A vanilla bean tied to a wire whisk with a recipe for Bavarian Cream or a vanilla bean packed in a pretty ceramic crock filled with fine granulated fruit sugar.

Tuck some wooden spoons in the pocket of a coverall apron; package a French lettuce basket or a plastic lettuce spinner with a tightly corked, wax-sealed bottle of your homemade salad dressing or a recipe tag for same. Or forget the salad dressing and include a pepper mill and a jar of Java or Tellichery peppercorns.

Bean pots, glazed pottery casseroles, onion soup bowls, ceramic canisters, stoneware loaf pans and pie plates all lend themselves to creative gift ideas. Team them with the specialty foods from your section of the country: a bag of paper shell pecans with a pie plate and your favorite recipe for Southern pecan pie; a bag of wild rice with the casserole and instructions for cooking it as the Indians do. Line an Italian bread basket with a kitchen towel and a matching pot holder and pack it with a set of measuring spoons, a measuring cup, a wooden spoon, a pastry board, and rolling pin cover. Tie on a hand-written recipe for crisp-crusted Italian bread. Fill a canvas shopping bag with those indispensable little kitchen gadgets—an apple corer, a pair of tongs, a butter ball maker, a melon ball cutter, a cucumber slicer, vegetable peelers, wire whisks, an egg slicer, a corkscrew, a can opener, and so on. Top it with a bunch of fresh garden flowers.

The ideas for culinary gifts with that personal touch are unlimited and the joy of giving need not be limited to the holiday season or for special occasions. It can, for those who take pleasure in giving, be at any time of the year and for no other reason than a token of admiration and affection.

5

Bake-and-Take
Breads, Cakes, and Pies

There's a lot of eating pleasure in a loaf of quick bread, some flaky baking powder biscuits, a batch of homemade doughnuts, or a pan of corn muffins; but as far as I am concerned, nothing can surpass the honest goodness of a loaf of homemade yeast bread, bursting with whole grain goodness and other natural wholesome ingredients.

On a rainy Saturday morning when the children are home from school, bread-making can become a family affair, with each member kneading his own favorite ingredients into a basic dough. Seeds such as caraway, poppy, or sesame, or spices such as cardamom, nutmeg, or saffron, all make a nice change from the norm. After the dough rises in a warm corner of the kitchen comes the most fun of all—punching the dough down and shaping it in any one of a dozen different ways—into rolls or crescents or pinwheels, small round loaves, long braided loaves, or the traditional loaf pan shape. Then comes the rewarding aroma emanating from the oven as the bread bakes to golden perfection, filling the kitchen with old-fashioned warmth and goodness.

It's just as easy to make four loaves of yeast bread as one, and one loaf is equivalent to a dozen rolls. When the breads are completely cool, wrap the ones you don't need for immediate use tightly in aluminum foil or transparent freezer bags. Label and store in the freezer where they will retain all their original homebaked flavor for at least six months.

For gift-giving, the ways to package homebaked breads are as many as the different kinds of breads themselves. Baskets and wicker trays of all shapes and sizes can be lined with a colorful napkin and filled with baked goods. Then there are wooden products galore, from a wooden hot rack to a French bread tray to a decorative bread board with a loaf of bread or some rolls on top. Plastic trays are good too. And those individual plastic or china snack plates are perfect for some warm cupcakes or rolls and a jar of your home-made jelly. Containers can be as inexpensive as aluminum foil pans all the way up the dollar scale to an electric bread or roll warmer. Just keep in mind, when your eye spots a lovely container that might strain your purse strings, that it is the thought that counts, not how much. It's how good it is rather than how expensive, and no product from the home kitchen is as rewarding to give and more warmly received by host or hostess than a loaf of homemade bread, or biscuits.

All bread gifts should be overwrapped in transparent film and ribbon-tied. Tuck in a fresh garden rose or a sprig of greenery or attach a few colorful baubles.

QUICK BREADS

CRISP CORN DOLLARS

1 cup cornmeal   1¾–2 cups boiling water
1 teaspoon salt   Butter
¼ teaspoon sugar

Preheat the oven to 450°. In a mixing bowl combine the cornmeal, salt, and sugar. Gradually stir in enough boiling water to make a batter about the same consistency as a heavy pancake batter.

Butter a rimmed baking sheet generously and put it in the hot oven until the butter sizzles. Remove pan (careful!) and pour the batter onto the hot sheet in little cakes about the size of silver dollars. Return the pan to the hot oven and bake for 15 minutes, or until the corn dollars are lightly browned. Serve hot.

Makes about 36 corn dollars.

BENNE BISCUITS

2 cups flour   5 tablespoons to 1 cup ice water
1 teaspoon salt   1 cup roasted sesame seeds
¼ teaspoon cayenne   Coarse salt (optional)
¾ cup shortening

In mixing bowl combine flour, salt, and cayenne. Cut in shortening with a pastry blender or two knives until mixture looks like coarse crumbs. With a fork stir in ice water to make a pie crust dough.

Roll pastry out thinly on lightly floured surface and sprinkle half the dough with sesame seeds that have been roasted in a shallow pan in 350° oven for about 20 minutes. Fold plain dough over the sesame seeds and again roll dough out thinly.

Cut into small wafers. Place wafers on ungreased baking sheets and bake in a 300° oven for 20–25 minutes. Remove from oven and, if desired, sprinkle with coarse salt, but do taste before doing this.

Pack into containers with tight-fitting lids.

Makes several dozen biscuits.

DUBLIN SCONES

2 cups all-purpose flour
1 teaspoon baking soda
1 teaspoon cream of tartar
½ teaspoon salt

½ cup shortening
½ cup seedless raisins or currants
¾ cup milk

In a mixing bowl combine the flour, soda, cream of tartar, and salt. Add the shortening and, using a pastry blender or two knives, cut the shortening into the flour mixture until it looks like coarse meal. Stir in raisins or currants.

Dump in the milk all at once and stir gently with a fork until the dough holds together. With hands, gather dough into a ball, turn it out onto a lightly floured board, and knead gently with floured fingers about 12 kneading strokes. Roll dough out on floured surface into a circle ½ inch thick and cut into eight pie-shaped wedges with a floured knife.

Place wedges about 1 inch apart on a baking sheet and bake in a 400° oven for 15 minutes.

Makes 8 scones.

BANANA-ORANGE NUT BREAD

6 cups biscuit mix
1½ cups light brown sugar
½ cup all-purpose flour
1 cup orange juice

4 ripe bananas, mashed
2 eggs, lightly beaten
2 cups scissor-cut dates
1 cup chopped walnuts or pecans

In a large mixing bowl or bowl of an electric beater combine biscuit mix, sugar, and flour. Add orange juice, bananas, and eggs and beat until well blended. Stir in dates and nuts.

Oil 4 1-pound coffee cans or 2 9 x 5 x 3-inch loaf pans, or half of each, and divide the dough into them. Bake in a preheated 350° oven for 50 minutes for coffee cans; 55–60 minutes for rectangular loaves.

Remove bread from oven and loosen sides with a spatula. Remove loaves from pans to cool. When cool, return gift breads to decorated coffee cans, cover with plastic tops, and gift-wrap.

DATE BREAD

1 pound pitted dates	¾ cup brown sugar
1 cup chopped walnuts	1 teaspoon vanilla
1 cup boiling water	1 egg
⅓ cup butter	2 cups all-purpose flour
5 tablespoons cold water	1 teaspoon baking powder
1 teaspoon baking soda	½ teaspoon salt

In a large mixing bowl combine the dates, nuts, boiling water, and butter. Beat until the butter is broken into small pieces. Add cold water; stir in soda, brown sugar, vanilla, egg, and flour. Add the baking powder and salt and beat until well blended.

Spoon batter into an oiled 8½ x 4½-inch loaf pan and bake in a 350° oven for about 1 hour, or until loaf tests done. Remove loaf from pan to cool on rack.

This fruit bread keeps moist for several weeks if wrapped in foil and stored in the refrigerator. It also freezes well.

HAWAIIAN NUT BREAD

3½ cups all-purpose flour	6 tablespoons butter
4 teaspoons baking powder	1½ cups brown sugar
½ teaspoon baking soda	2 eggs
½ teaspoon salt	1 1-pound can crushed pineapple
1 cup chopped macadamia nuts	

In mixing bowl combine the flour, baking powder, baking soda, salt, and nuts.

In another mixing bowl cream together the butter and sugar. Beat in eggs, one at a time, and continue to beat until mixture is smooth. Stir in half the flour mixture. Stir in pineapple and juice, then stir in remaining flour mixture.

Divide the batter into 2 1-pound loaf pans and bake in a 350° oven for 50–60 minutes, or until bread tests done. Let loaves cool for 5 minutes, then turn out onto racks to cool completely.

ROSETTES OR SWEDISH SOCKERSTRUVOR

To make these fragile fried cakes you will need a rosette iron. When you find a source for these, buy several—one for yourself and some to put aside for giving. Take care of your rosette iron as you would your omelet pan. Never wash it. Put it in the oil to gradually heat along with the oil and when finished, leave it in the oil until cooled. Simply wipe off the oil with paper towels and store it in a plastic bag.

1 cup milk   *2 eggs*
1 cup flour   *Shortening or oil for frying*
1 tablespoon sugar   *Confectioners' sugar*
Pinch salt

Put all the batter ingredients—the milk, flour, sugar, salt, and eggs—in container of an electric blender and blend on low speed until smooth, stopping to stir down sides of container a couple of times. Pour the batter into a small dish about ½ inch deep.

Heat 1–2 cups oil in a small skillet or mini-fryer to about 360°, or until a cube of bread browns in 1 minute. Dip the hot rosette iron into the batter up to but not over the edge of the iron. Lower the batter-coated iron into the hot oil and fry until the rosette is a delicate brown. If it browns in 12–15 seconds the oil is the perfect temperature; if not, adjust heat accordingly.

Raise the rosette iron out of the oil and tip it sideways to drain off any fat trapped between the iron and the fried cake. Remove the rosette from the iron with the help of a two-tined fork to paper towels to drain. Repeat until all batter is used. Serve warm sprinkled with confectioners' sugar as a crisp accompaniment to ice cream or fruit dessert, or for breakfast, or with tea or coffee.

Makes 80 rosettes.

Store them unsugared in a tight container in a dry place. They will keep crisp and fresh for many weeks but are best heated for a few minutes in a 250° oven. Sprinkle with confectioners' sugar just before serving.

A charming hostess gift would be a rosette iron packaged with a colorful kitchen towel or pot holder and an outsized ceramic salt shaker filled with confectioners' sugar. Be sure to attach the recipe for rosettes and care instructions for the iron.

WHOLE GRAIN BREADS

None of the traditional sweet egg breads that are part of the holiday season are included in this chapter. Here are recipes for our daily bread made primarily of whole grain cereals. They are better in flavor and more nutritious than any you can buy and completely free of chemical preservatives. An honest loaf needs no additives to prevent mold or staleness. With the right proportion of liquid, butter, sugar, and grain it remains fresh in the refrigerator for a couple of weeks and in the freezer for months.

Making bread is truly child's play! Anyone can master the art by knowing a little about what makes the dough rise, and by keeping in mind the following proportions of flour, liquid, sugar, salt, shortening, and yeast. For each loaf of bread you need:

YEAST: *1 envelope active dry yeast or 1 compressed yeast cake.* The yeast is a living plant and is responsible for making the dough rise. Care must be taken not to destroy it by using liquid that is too hot.

SALT: *1 teaspoon* for flavor.

SUGAR: *1 tablespoon* to furnish food for the yeast plants.

SHORTENING: *2 tablespoons* to give elasticity to the cells that develop in the mixture of flour and water. It also improves the keeping quality and makes a tender crust.

LIQUID: *1 cup milk or water.* Water makes a crustier loaf.

FLOUR: *About 3 cups.* Some wheat flour is necessary in all yeast breads to provide the network of cells that hold the gas produced by the yeast.

First let's make a basic recipe for two loaves of bread or one loaf and one dozen rolls. The recipe may be doubled when it is as practical for you to make four loaves as one—one to eat and three to give!

BASIC WHITE OAT BREAD WITH A
CRISP CRUST AND TENDER CRUMB

2 envelopes active dry yeast
½ cup lukewarm water
½ stick butter (4 tablespoons)
1 cup milk
2 teaspoons salt

2 cups quick-cooking oats
2 tablespoons sugar
About 4 cups all-purpose flour
½ cup cool water

Soften the yeast in the lukewarm water for 5 minutes, then stir until blended.

In saucepan heat the butter and milk until milk is steaming and butter is almost melted.

In mixing bowl put salt, oats, and sugar. If you have an electric beater put it to good use. Add hot milk mixture and stir until blended. Stir in 1 cup of the flour and the ½ cup cool water. This will reduce the temperature of the dough to make it safe to add the yeast. If the dough were too hot it would kill the yeast and your bread would not rise. As an extra precaution, stick a finger into the dough to make sure it is lukewarm, then stir in the yeast mixture. Beat in enough remaining flour to make a stiff batter.

Empty the batter out onto a well-floured surface and knead in just enough additional flour to make a dough that does not stick to the hands but is still soft. (Too much flour will make the bread dry.)

Shape the dough into a ball and put in an oiled bowl. Turn the ball over and around to oil the entire surface, cover with a towel, and let rise in a warm spot until double in bulk, about 1½ hours.

Punch dough down and turn it onto a floured board. Cut dough in half and knead each half until smooth and elastic. Then shape into a loaf as follows: Flatten dough into a rectangle about 1 inch thick. Fold each end of the rectangle toward the center and press down firmly. Then fold sides to center and pinch the center fold together.

Place each loaf, seam side down, in oiled 9 x 4-inch bread pan, cover loaves with a towel, and let rise until the sides of the bread reach the top of the pans and the center is rounded, about 1 hour.

Bake in a 375° oven for 45–50 minutes.

Once you have mastered the feel of the dough you can make endless variations—substituting bran, buckwheat, cornmeal, wheat germ, cornflakes for the oats, and adding mashed vegetables or seeds or dried fruit for different flavors and textures.

For 1 Loaf and 1 Dozen Rolls: Shape half the dough into a loaf as above. Knead the other half until smooth and elastic and divide into twelve portions. Shape each portion into a round roll. Place the rolls 2 inches apart on an oiled baking sheet, cover, and let rise until double in bulk, about 45 minutes. Bake at 375° for 20 minutes, or until golden brown.

Whole Wheat Bread: Use ¼ cup brown sugar and 2 tablespoons molasses in place of the granulated sugar; use whole wheat flour in place of half or all the all-purpose flour.

Swedish Rye Bread: Use brown sugar in place of white. Omit the oats and use half rye flour and half all-purpose flour for a total of 5–6 cups. Add 2 tablespoons caraway seeds to the batter.

Vienna Bread: Shape the dough into two long, thin loaves. Place several inches apart on oiled baking sheet and cut gashes on top of the loaves about 3 inches apart and 1 inch deep. When doubled in bulk, brush loaves with lightly beaten egg white before baking. About 10 minutes before loaves are browned, remove from oven, brush again with egg white, and sprinkle with coarse salt. Continue baking for 10 minutes.

Grissini or Bread Sticks: Roll half the dough into a rectangle about 8 inches long and ¼ inch thick. Cut it into strips ½ inch wide. Roll strips on floured surface with palms of the hands into sticks and place on oiled baking sheet. Cover and let rise until double in bulk, about 20 minutes. Bake at 375° for 15–20 minutes. For a crisp or seed-covered crust, brush with beaten eggs and sprinkle with poppy seeds or sesame seeds.

Poppy Seed Bubbles or Braids: For the bread, add 2 tablespoons poppy seeds to the batter. When the dough is smooth and elastic, cut in half. Shape each half into 25 equal pieces and form each piece into a ball.

Melt a stick of butter in a saucepan. Brush 2 8-inch square pans with butter. Dip each ball into the melted butter and arrange in the pans in rows of five across each way. Cover and let rise until double in bulk. Bake in 350° oven for 35–40 minutes.

For the braids, cut each half into three equal parts and roll each part into a long rope. Pinch three of the ropes together at one end, braid them together, and secure at the other end. Brush the braids with lightly beaten egg white and sprinkle each with about 1 tablespoon poppy seeds. When double in bulk, about 1 hour, bake in a 350° oven for 35–40 minutes.

HONEY WHEAT BREAD

1 cup plain granola	2 envelopes active dry yeast
½ cup honey	3 cups warm water
¼ cup light brown sugar	5 cups whole wheat flour
1 teaspoon salt	2½–3 cups all-purpose flour

In large mixing bowl combine granola, honey, sugar, salt, yeast, and water and stir until all ingredients are moistened. Gradually stir in 3 cups of the wheat flour and beat for 2 minutes. Stir in remaining wheat flour and enough all-purpose flour to make a soft dough.

Turn dough out onto a lightly floured board and knead for 5–8 minutes, or until dough is smooth and elastic. Place dough smooth side down in an oiled bowl and turn dough to oil it on all sides. Cover with waxed paper and let rise in a warm place until double in bulk, 1–1½ hours. Punch down and cut in half. Pat each half into a rectangle, pressing out any bubbles of air trapped in the dough. Shape each into a loaf and place in oiled 9 x 5-inch bread pan. Cover pans and let bread rise until almost doubled, about 1 hour. Bake in a 350° oven for 45–50 minutes.

DARK PUMPERNICKEL BREAD

1 tablespoon butter
1 tablespoon cornmeal
2 envelopes active dry yeast
2½ cups lukewarm water
⅓ cup molasses
1 tablespoon salt
2 tablespoons salad oil

2 1-ounce squares unsweetened
  chocolate, melted
1 cup 100% bran cereal
1½ cups rye flour
1½ cups whole wheat flour
2 tablespoons caraway seeds
3½–4 cups all-purpose flour

Butter a baking sheet and sprinkle with cornmeal. Soften yeast in ½ cup of the lukewarm water.

In a mixing bowl combine remaining water, molasses, salt, oil, chocolate, and bran cereal and stir until blended. Stir in rye and whole wheat flour and the caraway seeds. Add the yeast mixture and gradually beat in enough all-purpose flour to make a rather sticky dough.

Turn dough out on lightly floured board and knead until smooth. Cover with waxed paper and let rise until double in bulk, about 1½ hours. Punch down and again knead until smooth, but keep the dough soft in consistency. Cut dough in half. Shape each half into a round or oval loaf and place them at least 4 inches apart on a baking sheet. Cover with a towel and let rise for about 45 minutes, or until almost double in size, then bake in a 375° oven for 45–50 minutes.

SWEDISH RYE BREAD

3 cups rye flour
1 tablespoon crushed anise seeds
2 envelopes active dry yeast
2¼ cups lukewarm water

½ cup honey
2 tablespoons soft butter
1 tablespoon salt
3½–4 cups all-purpose flour

In mixing bowl combine 2 cups of the rye flour, the anise seeds, yeast, water, honey, butter, and salt. Beat on low speed for about 2 minutes to a smooth batter. Add remaining rye flour and 1 cup of the all-purpose flour and beat at medium speed for another 2 minutes.

With a wooden spoon stir in enough additional all-purpose flour to make a very soft dough. Turn dough out onto lightly floured surface and knead until smooth and elastic, adding a little more flour if necessary to keep the dough from being sticky. Oil surface of the dough, cover with waxed paper, and let rise until double in bulk, about 1½ hours. Punch dough down and knead again until dough is smooth. Divide dough into three parts and shape each part into a round, smooth ball. Place in oiled 1½-quart round or rectangular bowls or pans, cover, and let rise until almost doubled in bulk, about 45 minutes. Bake in a 375° oven for 35–40 minutes, or until loaves sound hollow when tapped. Cool on racks.

This makes a great gift for dad on Father's Day or for an after-the-game get together.

EGG BREAD OR BRIOCHE

One of my favorite hostess gifts is a loaf of egg bread made into traditional brioche shapes or baked in a loaf. Thinly sliced and toasted in a low oven, it makes divine melba-type toast. Reheated and buttered while warm, both the brioche and the sliced bread are nothing short of heavenly.

2 envelopes active dry yeast	6 whole eggs
½ cup lukewarm water	3½–4 cups flour
1 teaspoon sugar	2 sticks butter, at room
½ teaspoon salt	temperature (1 cup)
¼ cup sugar	

Soften yeast in the lukewarm water with the 1 teaspoon sugar. In mixing bowl combine the salt, ¼ cup sugar, and eggs. Beat until eggs are fluffy and sugar and salt are dissolved. Beat in 2 cups of the flour, then stir in the yeast.

Divide butter into chunks and add to yeast mixture. Add another cup flour and beat well. Work in 1 more cup flour, or enough to make a soft dough. Do not add more of this last cup of flour than is absolutely necessary.

Turn dough out onto lightly floured board and knead the dough until it is smooth and silky. Cover with a towel and let rise for 1½ hours. Punch dough down and cut in half. Shape half into a loaf and place seam side down in oiled 8 x 4-inch bread pan. From the other half pinch off twelve little pieces about the size of a hazelnut and set aside. Divide remaining dough into twelve pieces and form into smooth balls. Place each ball in an oiled, fluted brioche pan or custard cup. Cut a small, deep cross in the center of each and insert one of the tiny balls into the cross.

Cover the loaf and the brioche with a towel and let rise in a warm spot. The brioche will be ready to bake in about 20 minutes, the loaves in about 40. Bake the brioche at 375° for 20–25 minutes, the loaf for 40–45 minutes.

Remove from pans while hot and cool. When cool, wrap in protective paper or plastic bags and freeze.

To reheat, tuck them into a small roast-in bag and bake at 300° for 30 minutes if still frozen; if at room temperature, 10–15 minutes is sufficient.

BAGELS

2 *envelopes active dry yeast*   1½ *cups lukewarm water*
4¼–4½ *cups sifted all-purpose*   3 *tablespoons sugar*
    flour   1 *tablespoon salt*

In large mixer bowl combine yeast and 1¾ cups of the flour. Combine water, sugar, and salt; add to yeast mixture. Beat at low speed of electric mixer for 30 seconds, scraping sides of bowl constantly. Beat 3 minutes at high speed. By hand, stir in enough of the remaining flour to make a moderately stiff dough. Turn out on lightly floured surface and knead until smooth. Cover and let rest 15 minutes.

Cut into twelve portions and shape into small balls. Punch a hole in center of each with floured finger. Pull gently to enlarge hole, working each bagel into uniform shape. Cover; let rise 20 minutes.

In large kettle, combine 1 gallon water and 1 tablespoon sugar. Bring to boiling. Reduce temperature to simmering and cook bagels four to five at a time for 7 minutes, turning once. Drain. Place on ungreased baking sheets and bake in 375° oven for 30–35 minutes.

Makes 12 bagels.

Bagels are fun to give with the traditional thinly sliced salmon and a crock of cream cheese.

BISCUIT BUBBLE BREAD

When time is short and you want to take a yeasty sweet bread along with you when you visit a friend, try this easy one made from refrigerator biscuits.

6 *ounces cream cheese*   1 *teaspoon ground cinnamon*
2 10-*biscuit packages refrigerator*   ½ *teaspoon ground nutmeg*
    biscuits   ½ *stick butter, melted*
½ *cup light brown sugar*   ½ *cup chopped pecans*

Cream the cheese, cut into twenty pieces and form each piece into a small ball.

Combine sugar, cinnamon and nutmeg.

On lightly floured board roll out each biscuit into a round about 3 inches in diameter. Place a ball of cheese in the center of each and sprinkle with 1 teaspoon of the sugar mixture.

Pour half the melted butter into a 5-cup ring mold and swirl the mold to coat it lightly with the butter. Sprinkle mold with half the nuts and half the remaining sugar mixture. Arrange half the biscuit rolls in the mold, seam side up. Pour over remaining butter and repeat the layers.

Bake in a preheated 375° oven for 20–25 minutes, or until the bread is nicely browned. Cool for about 5 minutes before inverting it onto a serving plate.

For immediate gift-giving, wash the mold, return the loaf to it, over-wrap, and include the mold in your gift along with the bread. Reheat the loaf if you wish before serving in a 250° oven.

BAKE-AND-TAKE CAKES

Every good cook has her favorite recipes for cakes, any of which would make a mouth-watering gift for an acquaintance or friend. When cool, frost the cake, sprinkle with chopped nuts or chocolate curls, or decorate with frosting pressed through a small fluted pastry tube. Insert it in an attractive basket with a handle. It need not fit the basket perfectly. If it is too large, pack tissue around it, cover the cake and basket with transparent film, and decorate the handle with greens or flowers or a ribbon bow.

Cake batters may actually be baked right in wicker baskets providing the straw is raw and not varnished. Soak the basket in cold water for a few minutes while you make the cake batter. Then dry the basket and line it with aluminum foil. Fill two-thirds full of batter and bake until the cake tests done. Cool, frost, glaze or decorate.

My favorite gift cake is an old-fashioned pound cake sprinkled gener-ously with confectioners' sugar when cool. It is so delightfully simple, its keeping qualities are hard to beat, and it freezes well. It's lovely thinly sliced and served for tea or toasted and buttered for breakfast. Either way, team it with a jar of your homemade jam or jelly.

VICTORIAN POUND CAKE

2 sticks butter
1½ cups sugar
5 whole large eggs

1½ cups all-purpose flour
2 teaspoons vanilla
¼ teaspoon salt

In mixing bowl cream together butter and sugar until mixture is light and fluffy. Add eggs, one at a time, beating well after each addition. Gradually stir in the flour to make a smooth batter. Stir in vanilla and salt.

Spoon the batter into a 6-cup floured loaf pan and bake in a 325° oven for 1 hour, 20 minutes. Let cool for a few minutes, then turn out onto rack to cool.

When completely cool, wrap tightly in aluminum foil or transparent freezer wrap, label, and freeze.

BAKE-AND-TAKE PIES

Pies, too, make welcome gifts, and the different kinds are too numerous to include in this small book. Make them sweet or savory; make them with one crust or double crusted. Sprinkle the sweet ones with confectioners' sugar or bake on a meringue topping; garnish the savory ones with parsley or radish roses or the thin peeled skin from a ripe tomato curled around petal-fashion into a flower in full bloom. Make the leaves out of sweet basil, dill sprigs, or watercress.

Package pies as you would cakes—in handled baskets or in a traditional New England covered pie basket that holds two pies—one might be sweet and one savory.

Another excellent pie carrier is readily available and inexpensive. It has a clear styrene top that clamps onto the plate in which the pie was baked. It protects and keeps the pie fresh, too. The top handle lets you carry it to picnics, parties, and is useful for transportable gift-giving.

No way can I avoid putting in my two cents' worth of pie by way of a great new recipe for a savory appetizer baked in a flaky crust. From then on, as a pie baker, you're on your own.

CHILI QUICHE

Pastry for a 1-crust pie
2 tablespoons butter
4 green onions, including tender
green tops, chopped
1 4-ounce can chopped green
chilies

8 ounces Swiss or Gruyère cheese,
shredded
4 egg yolks
¼ teaspoon paprika
1½ cups cream

Line pie plate with pastry. Line pastry with waxed paper and weigh down paper with a cup of peas, beans, or rice. Bake in a 450° oven for 8 minutes. Remove from oven, save peas or rice, and discard paper. Let cool.

In a small skillet melt butter and in it sauté the onions and chilies for 3 minutes, or until onion is tender. Spread mixture in bottom of partially baked crust. Sprinkle cheese on top.

Combine egg yolks, paprika, and cream. Pour over cheese and bake the pie in a 325° oven for 40 minutes. Serve hot, warm, or cool.

Reheats well in a slow oven.

6

Sugar and Spice and All Things Nice... Holiday Fruitcakes, Puddings, and Mincemeats

November is none too early to begin thinking about Christmas, and it is in the making, the baking, the creating of your own gifts that the true spirit of the season is captured.

It's time to think about those special holiday foods which either need time to age and ripen or will stay safe and flavorful in the freezer until needed. It's time to think about imaginative ways to package gifts from the home kitchen so that the container itself will "keep on giving" long after the contents have been savored.

As Betty Chancellor said so charmingly in a Christmas cookbook she wrote for children . . .

"Begin making gifts at a quarter to June, and when it's half-past November, gifts should be finished and ready to wrap."

So the jams and jellies we made in June, the pickles we made in October, and the special holiday sweets we're going to make now, will be ready at half-past the month to wrap and send on their way, knowing that their most important ingredient is love.

There is still time to shop for containers for the gifts you will carry with you when you visit friends to say "Happy Holidays." The containers may be anything from an empty can or box to an expensive tray or decanter. By adding a personal touch to every gift you give you are saying, "This is especially for you."

For the men on your list, you might plan on a cocktail shaker or a wooden salad bowl heaping with cookies, or a set of six glasses or brandy snifters, each filled with a different kind of candy or spiced nut.

The container in which you package the gifts from your kitchen can make the gift into whatever you wish it to be—a token of your friendship, a thank-you to a good neighbor, a gift for remembrance, or a generous contribution to a loved one's life.

The recipes in this chapter are for sweet treats that can be made well in advance of the holiday season. Some, such as fruitcakes and plum puddings, often kept from one year to the next, need time to age; others keep well if stored in tightly covered containers; and still others need to be frozen to retain their freshness.

HOLIDAY FRUITCAKES

Christmas wouldn't be Christmas without cakes and puddings bursting with sugar, spices, and fruits, and fragrant with sherry, wine, or brandy.

The batter for fruitcakes can be baked in almost any shape or size of container that can be lined with aluminum foil or plain brown wrapping paper. Ring molds, tube pans, loaf pans, melon molds, fluted molds are all good, and for gift-giving, empty 1-pound coffee or shortening cans hold just about 1 pound of your favorite fruitcake. Ordinary clay or ceramic flower pots may also be used both for baking and for giving.

When the cakes are cool, remove them from the cans or pots while you decorate the containers with gift paper, decals, gold trim, and so on. Glaze the tops with confectioners' sugar frosting and decorate with bits of candied fruits and nuts.

Wrap the decorated cakes in transparent film, return them to the cans or pots, and top with a colorful bow. If the cans are the kind with plastic lids, replace them, by all means, before attaching the bow. Reserve the containers with the plastic tops for fruitcakes that you are going to ship by parcel post or air.

For individual servings of fruitcake, bake the batter in cupcake pans lined with fluted foil cups. When cool, package them on lacquered trays or earthenware cake plates, in large glass canisters or clear plastic boxes decorated with decals. Overwrap if necessary and attach some baubles and bows.

The fruits and nuts specified in a fruitcake recipe can be changed providing the total number of cups remains the same. Spices may be varied in the same way.

To Bake Fruitcakes: Long slow cooking is used in baking fruitcakes, generally 250–300°. One-pound cakes will take about 1½ hours; large ones 3–4 hours; while individual cupcake sizes will be done in 30–40 minutes. However, before removing any fruitcake from the oven be sure to insert a cake tester down through the center. If it comes out clean with no soft batter adhering to it, the cake is done.

For a greater volume, moist texture, and a shiny top, place a shallow pan of hot water on bottom shelf of the oven during the baking period.

Cool fruitcakes in the containers in which they were baked, then remove from containers to store and ripen.

To Store Fruitcakes: Wrap the cooled cakes tightly in aluminum foil and store in tightly closed container. Store at least a week before cutting and serving; when kept longer than that, open the foil every couple of weeks and moisten the cakes with a little wine, rum, or brandy.

To Cut Fruitcakes: If the fruitcake is chilled before cutting, it will cut more easily. Use a sharp, sturdy knife.

RICH DARK FRUITCAKE

This fruitcake originated in England. Traditionally it is covered with a 1-inch layer of almond paste, then lightly iced with confectioners' sugar frosting and decorated with bits of glacéd cherries, citron, and almonds.

2 *pounds golden raisins*	1 *teaspoon baking soda*
5 *pounds seedless raisins*	2 *teaspoons double-acting baking*
2 *pounds currants*	*powder*
1 *pound candied cherries*	2 *pounds butter*
1 *pound whole almonds*	4 *cups brown sugar, firmly packed*
½ *pound citron*	12 *eggs, lightly beaten*
½ *pound mixed candied orange*	½ *cup molasses*
and lemon peel	½ *cup orange juice*
10 *cups all-purpose flour*	½ *cup sherry*
1 *tablespoon ground cinnamon*	¼ *cup vanilla*
1 *teaspoon each ground cloves,*	*Brandy*
nutmeg, allspice	

Wash raisins and currants and, if dry, steam them in a colander over boiling water for 5 minutes. Set aside. Separate candied cherries. Blanch almonds and remove skins. Slice citron, orange, and lemon peel thinly.

In large bowl combine all fruits and nuts together with 1 cup of the flour. Combine remaining flour with the spices, soda, and baking powder. In large container cream butter until soft. Gradually beat in sugar and beat together until mixture is light and fluffy. Stir in eggs and molasses. Gradually stir in flour mixture alternately with the orange juice, sherry, and vanilla. Fold in fruits and nuts.

Line 8 2-pound loaf pans (8 x 4 x 3 inches) or 6-cup capacity molds with heavy brown paper. Butter paper generously. Fill the pans or molds almost full of batter.

Bake in a very slow 250° oven for 2–2½ hours, or until cake tester inserted in center comes out clean.

Remove cakes from pans to cake racks and, when cool, pour about 2 ounces brandy over each cake. Wrap each cake in aluminum foil and store in tightly covered tins. Moisten occasionally (about once a month) with brandy. Cakes will keep from one Christmas to the next.

Makes 8 2-pound loaves.

Recipe may be halved.

VIRGINIA WHITE FRUITCAKE

Bake half this fruit-filled batter in a tube pan and the rest of it in 1-pound coffee cans for gift giving.

½ pound butter, softened
2 cups sugar
6 eggs, lightly beaten
5 cups all-purpose flour
1 small coconut, grated, or 2 cups
*   shredded moist coconut*
1 cup coarsely chopped walnuts
1 cup coarsely chopped pecans
1 cup finely cut candied citron

1 pound golden raisins
½ pound candied pineapple,
*   chopped*
½ pound candied cherries,
*   chopped*
2 teaspoons baking powder
1 teaspoon salt
1 cup sherry or cognac

Cream together butter and sugar until mixture is light and fluffy. Beat in eggs. Mix 2 cups of the flour with the coconut, nuts, citron, raisins, pineapple, and cherries. Combine remaining flour, baking powder, and salt and stir into egg mixture alternately with the sherry or cognac. Fold in fruit mixture.

Line 10-inch pan with oiled waxed paper and fill the pan with half the batter. Line 4 1-pound coffee cans with oiled waxed paper and fill with remaining batter. Bake in a 275° oven for 30 minutes; lower heat to 250° and continue to bake for about 3 hours for the large cake, about 1½ hours for the small cakes, or until the cakes test done.

GOLDEN GOOD LUCK FRUITCAKE

There is a superstition that anyone who eats a piece of fruitcake on each of the days between Christmas and New Year's, and makes a wish on the first mouthful, will be blessed with good luck and fortune in the following year.

¾ cup golden seedless raisins
1½ cups blanched almonds,
    slivered
½ cup pistachio nuts or pecans
1½ cups diced candied pineapple
1 cup moist shredded coconut
½ pound candied cherries, halved
½ pound candied lemon peel,
    chopped
½ pound candied orange peel,
    chopped

¼ cup citron, slivered
2 cups all-purpose flour
1 cup butter (2 sticks)
1 cup sugar
5 eggs, lightly beaten
1 teaspoon salt
1 teaspoon baking powder
½ cup orange juice
2 teaspoons vanilla

In a large mixing bowl combine all fruit, nuts, and peel with ½ cup of the flour.

In another large container cream butter and sugar until light and fluffy. Beat in eggs. Combine remaining flour with salt and baking powder and stir into egg mixture alternately with the orange juice and vanilla. Stir in floured fruits and nuts.

Spoon batter into 1 large pan or several small ones that have been lined with brown paper and well oiled. Bake in a 275° oven for about 4 hours for the large cake, less for the smaller ones. Test with cake tester before removing from the oven.

When cool, moisten with wine or brandy, wrap, and store in a cool place.

DATE NUT FRUITCAKE

4 eggs, separated
1½ cups all-purpose flour
1½ cups sugar
Pinch salt
1 teaspoon baking powder
1 pound walnuts

1 pound Brazil nuts
2 pounds pitted dates
1 pound candied cherries
½ pound candied pineapple,
    chopped

Beat egg yolks until thick and lemon-colored. Combine the flour, sugar, salt, and baking powder and sprinkle over whole nuts and fruits. Add egg yolks; mix well. Beat egg whites until stiff but not dry; fold into fruit mixture. Pour into greased and floured 2-pound loaf pans. Bake in slow 250° oven for 2 hours.

Makes approximately 8 pounds of fruitcake, or 4 2-pound loaves.

HOLIDAY GIFT CAKE

This recipe makes very rich loaf cakes, more like a confection than a conventional fruitcake.

2 cups red candied cherries	6 cups whole Brazil nuts
2 cups green candied cherries	6 cups pecan halves
1 cup cognac	3 cups flour
1 cup chopped candied citron	3 cups sugar
1 cup chopped candied lemon or orange peel	2 teaspoons baking powder
	1 teaspoon salt
2 cups seedless golden raisins	12 eggs
2 pounds whole pitted dates	1 tablespoon vanilla

In a small bowl combine red and green cherries. Pour the cognac over them and let them soak for ½ hour, stirring occasionally. While they are soaking, prepare your pans. Use 9 x 4 x 3-inch loaf pans or a variety of copper molds or clean empty cans. Oil them and line with plain brown wrapping paper. Oil the paper well. Set aside.

Drain the cognac off the cherries and reserve.

In large preserving kettle combine cherries, citron, peel, raisins, dates, and nuts. Combine flour, sugar, baking powder, and salt. Sprinkle over the fruit and nut mixture and toss lightly.

Beat eggs until light and fluffy. Stir in the vanilla and pour over the fruit and nut mixture. Mix just enough to moisten all the dry ingredients. It will be a very stiff fruit-filled mixture. Spoon it into prepared pans, leveling the top with the back of a spoon.

Bake in a 300° oven for 2½ hours, or until cakes test done. If batter is baked in smaller pans than the standard loaf pan the baking time will be shorter.

Remove cakes from oven, prick cakes deeply with a wooden pick, and spoon over each a little of the reserved cognac. When cool enough to handle, remove cakes and the paper lining to a rack to cool completely.

When cool, discard paper and wrap each cake tightly in aluminum foil with a double seal on top. Store in a cool place for at least three weeks before using. Open the packages each week and spoon a few teaspoons of cognac over each.

Makes 4 cakes.

Recipe may be halved.

PLUM PUDDINGS

In England, plum puddings are made on Stir-Up Day or the fourth Sunday before Christmas so they will have time to age. There, as well as in many American homes, steamed fruit-and-nut puddings are the traditional flamboyant finale to festive holiday meals. Contrary to tradition, they need not be cooked in one large mold. Individual serving molds can be charmingly arranged in a circle on a footed cake plate, decorated with sprigs of holly, and blazed with brandy as effectively as the large pudding.

If making a large quantity of plum pudding, put the suet and fruit through the coarse blade of a meat grinder. It can save a lot of time.

TO COOK A PLUM PUDDING: Set it on a rack in a deep pot and add boiling water to come halfway up the sides of the mold; cover the pot and steam the pudding for 1–5 hours, depending on size of mold. Two-quart molds will need about 5 hours steaming; individual puddings about 1 hour. Remove molds from pot and, when cool enough to handle, remove puddings from molds and cool completely on a rack. Wrap tightly in foil and store in the refrigerator or freezer.

Plum puddings may be cooked in just about anything: a casserole, a Pyrex bowl, melon molds, deep decorative ring molds, empty cans, or custard cups. The molds must be securely covered, either with the cover of the mold itself or with aluminum foil. Tie on the foil-cover tightly with string.

Plum puddings are always served hot with hard sauce or a brandy rum-flavored pudding sauce, and they are usually brought to the table in a circle of flames.

To Reheat a Plum Pudding: If frozen, remove from freezer the evening before you plan to serve it. It may be either left in its foil wrapping and reheated in a 325° oven or it can be returned to the mold in which it was steamed, covered tightly, and steamed again for 1–2 hours.

To Blaze a Plum Pudding: Heat a little brandy or rum in a small saucepan to just lukewarm. Sprinkle the pudding with fine fruit sugar, pour the warm brandy over and around it, and set it aflame.

Let the flame burn out before serving.

To Gift-Package a Plum Pudding: Tuck in a small crock of hard sauce and attach instructions for reheating and flaming the pudding.

ROUND TABLE PLUM PUDDING

1 pound suet, ground
½ cup blanched almonds
½ cup currants
½ cup seedless raisins
½ cup golden raisins
½ cup chopped apple
¼ cup finely chopped candied orange rind
¼ cup finely chopped candied lemon rind
¼ cup slivered citron
½ cup chopped preserved ginger
¼ cup chopped dried figs

¼ cup chopped pitted dates
¼ cup candied cherries
1 cup brown sugar
½ teaspoon salt
1 teaspoon each cinnamon and nutmeg
½ teaspoon each clove and mace
Juice and grated rind of 1 orange
Juice and grated rind of 1 lemon
3 cups dark rum
1½ cups fine dry bread crumbs
¾ cup flour
6 eggs, beaten

Ten days before steaming the pudding, mix suet, nuts, fruit and rinds, sugar, salt, and spices in a large bowl. Moisten the mixture with the orange and lemon juice and 1 cup of the dark rum. Cover the bowl with a transparent film and marinate in the refrigerator for 10 days, adding a few tablespoons of rum and tossing the mixture each day.

The day the pudding is to be steamed, stir in the remaining rum, bread crumbs, flour, and eggs. Turn the batter into 2 well-buttered 1-quart molds, filling the molds three-quarters full. Tie aluminum foil over the molds and put them on a rack in a large kettle containing water which comes to 2 inches of the top of the mold. Cover kettle and simmer for 5 hours.

Makes 12 servings.

HOLIDAY PLUM PUDDING

½ cup all-purpose flour
4 cups fine bread crumbs (use a blender if you have one)
1 cup sugar
1 pound kidney suet, finely chopped
1 pound seedless raisins
1 cup currants
1 pound light golden raisins
1 cup slivered blanched almonds
1 cup coarsely chopped black walnuts
1 cup chopped mixed candied fruit peel

1 cup halved candied cherries
½ cup chopped candied lemon peel
1 tablespoon grated nutmeg
1 teaspoon ground mace
½ teaspoon each ground cloves, cinnamon, and ginger
1 teaspoon salt
8 eggs
½ cup milk
1 cup brandy
½ cup sherry or rum

In large mixing bowl combine flour, crumbs, sugar, suet, fruit, spices, and salt. Mix well. In another bowl beat eggs lightly and stir in milk, brandy, and sherry or rum. Stir egg mixture into fruit mixture.

Divide batter into 2 1½-quart bowls or molds, cover containers with waxed paper, then tie aluminum foil over tops and secure with string.

Set containers on a rack in a large pot of simmering water to come halfway up sides of container and simmer, covered, for about 6 hours, adding more water to the pot when needed. Cool, wrap, and refrigerate or store in a cool place.

To serve, steam for 1½ hours before turning out of mold, and serve flambéed with rum or brandy.

Makes 8 servings.

EGGLESS CHRISTMAS PUDDING

3½ cups flour
2 teaspoons cream of tartar
1 teaspoon salt
1 teaspoon baking soda
1 teaspoon ground cinnamon
½ teaspoon ground cloves
½ teaspoon ground mace

1 cup ground suet
1½ cups seedless raisins
1 cup currants
¼ cup chopped candied orange peel
1 cup molasses
1 cup milk

Sift together flour, cream of tartar, salt, baking soda, and spices. Mix together the suet, raisins, currants, orange peel, molasses, and milk; mix well. Add flour mixture a little at a time, blending well after each addition.

Spoon into an oiled 1½-quart ring mold or into 3 2-cup molds. Tie on aluminum foil to cover and steam: 4 hours for the large mold; 1 hour and 40 minutes for the smaller gift-sized molds.

Makes 9 servings; each of the small molds serves 3.

STEAMED BRAZIL NUT PUDDING

½ cup orange juice
1¾ cups seedless raisins
⅓ cup slivered citron
1 apple, peeled, cored, and
    chopped
1 tablespoon grated orange rind
2 eggs
1 cup unsulphured molasses
1 cup chopped Brazil nuts
½ cup ground suet

½ cup dry bread crumbs
½ cup all-purpose flour
1 teaspoon baking powder
½ teaspoon baking soda
¼ cup sugar
½ teaspoon salt
½ teaspoon ground cinnamon
¼ teaspoon ground allspice
¼ teaspoon ground cloves

Pour orange juice over raisins, citron, apple, and orange rind and set aside for 1 hour.

Beat eggs and molasses until well blended. Stir in nuts, suet, and bread crumbs. Combine flour, baking powder, soda, sugar, salt, and spices and stir into egg mixture. Add fruit and blend thoroughly.

Spoon into a buttered 2-quart pudding mold or casserole and cover with the cover of the mold or with aluminum foil.

Place mold on rack in a deep kettle and pour in boiling water to come halfway up sides of mold. Cover kettle and steam for 5 hours, adding more boiling water if necessary.

(Individual molds containing more than 1 cup of batter require about 2 hours steaming. Molds containing less than 1 cup of batter should be steamed for about 1 hour. Allow at least a ½-inch space between molds and the sides of the kettle.)

When cool enough to handle, remove from mold and wrap in aluminum foil. Store in refrigerator.

To reheat, place pudding in its foil wrappings in a 325° oven for 1 hour. Or you can return it to the mold in which it was originally steamed and steam it again for about 1 hour.

Makes 12 servings.

TRADITIONAL HARD SAUCE

1 cup butter (2 sticks)
2 cups confectioners' sugar
Pinch salt
2 tablespoons brandy or rum

Cream butter in a small bowl until soft. Gradually stir in sugar, salt, and rum or brandy. Beat the sauce until very light and creamy.

Pack the hard sauce into a pretty mold and refrigerate until hard. Remove from the mold and serve on a crystal plate garnished with a sprig of holly.

Or chill the sauce until hard, then roll into balls, using about 1 tablespoon for each. Freeze the balls on a small baking sheet; when frozen, pack into transparent freezer bags.

Makes about 2 cups.

Orange-flavored Curaçao or Triple Sec may be used in place of the rum or brandy, and finely grated orange and/or lemon rind may be added.

BRANDY SAUCE

½ cup honey
2 tablespoons boiling water
1 teaspoon butter
¼ cup brandy or rum

Combine honey, water, and butter and heat until butter is melted. Remove from heat, cool to lukewarm, and stir in the rum or brandy.

Makes about 1 cup.

MINCEMEATS

Mincemeat filling for pies, tarts, and turnovers may be made well in advance of Christmas, and when packed in quart jars makes a thoughtful gift for a busy neighbor or a working mother who has little time for holiday cooking. She may make time for a batch of cookies and some candies, but mincemeat would probably be the last item on her list to make because of the availability of very good commercially-packed mincemeat.

However, like all the other suggestions in this book, homemade mincemeat far outranks the commercial brands. One quart is just the right amount for a 9-inch pie.

MINCEMEAT

2 cups finely chopped cooked lean
    beef
3 cups chopped sour apple
2 cups seedless raisins
2 cups currants
1 cup finely slivered citron
1 cup chopped dried peaches

1 cup chopped suet
2 cups brown sugar
1 cup sweet cider
1 tablespoon each ground cloves,
    nutmeg, and cinnamon
2 teaspoons salt
1 cup beef broth

Combine all ingredients in large kettle. Bring to a boil and simmer for 1 hour. Seal while hot in clean hot jars.

    Makes about 3 quarts.

HONEYED MINCEMEAT

1 pound ground lean meat
1 pound ground suet
4 pounds apples, peeled, seeded,
    and chopped
2 pounds seedless raisins
2 pounds currants
½ pound chopped citron
2 tablespoons grated lemon rind

3 tablespoons grated orange rind
2 cups corn syrup
1 cup honey
2 cups sugar
1 teaspoon each ground cinnamon,
    ginger, and nutmeg
½ teaspoon ground cloves

Combine all ingredients. Bring to a simmer, cover, and cook for 30 minutes, stirring occasionally. Seal while hot in clean hot jars.

    Makes 5 quarts.

GREEN TOMATO MINCEMEAT

3 pounds green tomatoes
1 tablespoon salt
3 pounds tart apples, peeled, cored,
    and chopped
2 cups brown sugar
2 pounds seedless raisins

1 cup ground suet
½ cup vinegar
2½ tablespoons cinnamon
1 tablespoon nutmeg
1 tablespoon grated lemon rind
2 teaspoons ground cloves

Wash the tomatoes and put them through the medium blade of a food chopper. Mix the ground tomatoes with the salt and let stand for 1 hour.

Drain the tomatoes, add water just to cover, and bring to a boil. Simmer for 5 minutes, then drain. Add the remaining ingredients, bring to a boil, and simmer for 1 hour, stirring frequently. Seal in hot sterilized jars.

Makes 3 quarts.

7

Holiday Sweet Breads for Good Eating and for Giving

What would Christmas be without tradition? Every charming aspect of Christmas—the tree, the gifts, the turkey, old Santa himself—is a venerable tradition. In Sweden, where traditions are as thick as berries on a holly bush, there is a special tradition of making a Christmas bread on "little Christmas Eve" or December 23. The sugar-frosted loaf, garnished with Christmas greenery, is displayed on the table until Christmas morning, as a reminder of the hope that the next year's harvest will be a generous one.

Sweet yeasty egg breads have been closely identified with yuletide celebrations for centuries and today, in Europe and America, these breads continue to be an important part of holiday festivities. We don't have to wait until December 23 to make and bake them. If there's an ample freezer, they can be made many weeks before Christmas, tightly wrapped in aluminum foil, and frozen.

All the Christmas breads may be shaped into rolls rather than loaves. For rolls with soft sides, place balls of the fruit-and-nut-filled dough almost touching in greased, deep square or round pans. Let rise in a warm place for about 1 hour, or until doubled in bulk, and bake at 425° for 15 minutes, or until lightly browned. For crusty rolls, place well apart on greased baking sheets to rise, then bake in the same manner as for soft-sided rolls.

Sweet breads and rolls, unless they are to be frosted on top, are usually glazed with milk, unbeaten egg white mixed with 1 tablespoon cold water, or with lightly beaten egg yolk mixed with a little milk. Brush the tops with glaze just before baking and again a few minutes before taking them from the oven.

TRADITIONAL CHRISTMAS BREADS

PANNETONE DI NATALE (Italy)

1 envelope active dry yeast
¼ cup lukewarm water
1 tablespoon sugar
½ teaspoon salt
2½–3 cups all-purpose flour
2 large or 3 small eggs
¼ cup milk

⅔ cup soft butter
½ cup chopped candied fruit peel
1 cup seedless raisins
½ cup chopped candied citron
½ cup chopped blanched almonds
¼ cup chopped candied cherries
2 teaspoons vanilla

Soften yeast in water for 5 minutes, then stir until blended. In mixing bowl combine sugar, salt, and 1¼ cups flour. Stir in yeast and eggs, lightly beaten with the milk. Beat until batter is smooth. Add butter, fruit peel, raisins, citron, almonds, cherries, and vanilla and beat thoroughly until butter is blended into the batter. Beat in 1¼ cups flour and, with floured fingers, work in enough additional flour to make a soft dough that does not stick to fingers.

Turn dough out on lightly floured board and knead for about 2 minutes. Cover and let rise for 1½ hours, or until double in bulk. Punch dough down, shape into a loaf, and put into a greased small bread pan or ring mold. Let rise about 1 hour, or until double in bulk.

Preheat oven to 375°. Bake for 40 minutes, or until golden. While hot, frost with Thin Decorator's Frosting (see page 110).

Makes 1 loaf.

STOLLEN (Sweden)

Many of the Christmas breads are basically the same, but the proportion of fruit and nuts and the shapes often differ. Such is the case with stollen, which is in the form of a large Parker House roll.

1 envelope active dry yeast
2 tablespoons lukewarm water
1 cup milk
1 cup soft butter (2 sticks)
½ cup sugar
1 teaspoon salt
2 eggs, beaten
1 egg yolk, beaten

3 cups all-purpose flour
¾ cup seedless raisins
¼ cup finely shredded candied
    citron
¼ cup chopped candied cherries
¾ cup chopped nuts
2 tablespoons melted butter

Soften yeast in lukewarm water. Scald milk and stir in butter, sugar, and salt. Cool to lukewarm. Empty lukewarm milk mixture into mixing bowl and stir in yeast. Add eggs and enough flour to make a stiff batter. Beat well with a wooden spoon until dough almost blisters. Beat in raisins, citron, cherries, and nuts, then knead in additional flour to make a dough that is soft but not sticky.

Turn dough out onto lightly floured board and knead thoroughly. Cover and let rise for 1½ hours, or until double in bulk. Punch dough down and shape into two balls. Let rest for 10 minutes, then flatten each ball into an oval about ¾ inch thick. Brush surface of dough with melted butter and fold in half like large Parker House rolls. Pinch ends firmly together and place on greased baking sheet. Brush tops with melted butter and let rise for about 1 hour, or until double in bulk.

Preheat oven to 350°. Bake the stollen in the preheated oven for 35 minutes. When cool, brush with Thin Decorator's Frosting (see page 110) and decorate with large pieces of fruit and nuts.

Makes 2 loaves.

JULEKAKE (Norway)

¾ cup milk	½ cup melted butter (1 stick)
½ cup sugar	½ cup raisins
¼ teaspoon salt	¼ cup dried currants
1 envelope active dry yeast	4 ounces candied fruit
¼ cup warm water	2 cups all-purpose flour
½ teaspoon ground cardamom	1 egg yolk
1½ cups all-purpose flour	1 tablespoon water

Scald milk; pour into large bowl. Stir in sugar and salt. Cool to lukewarm.

Sprinkle yeast into warm water in small bowl; stir to dissolve.

Add cardamom, 1½ cups flour, and melted butter to milk mixture; add yeast mixture; beat well. Cover bowl with waxed paper and cloth. Let rise in warm place until doubled, about 1½ hours.

Punch down. Add raisins, currants, fruit, and 2 cups flour. Knead lightly until smooth and elastic. Put in greased bowl; cover and let rise in warm place until doubled, about 2 hours.

Grease large baking sheet. Punch down dough; shape into round ball, and place on baking sheet. Cover and let rise in warm place until almost doubled.

Beat egg yolk with water; brush over surface of dough. Bake in 350° oven for 30–40 minutes. If top gets too brown, cover with aluminum foil.

While still hot, spread with ½ cup confectioners' sugar mixed with 1 tablespoon hot water. Decorate with candied fruit.

Makes 1 loaf.

SPICY CHRISTMAS FRUIT BREAD (England)

½ cup shredded citron
½ cup chopped raisins
½ cup chopped blanched almonds
½ cup chopped candied cherries
1 tablespoon grated lemon rind
1 teaspoon ground cinnamon
½ teaspoon ground cloves
½ teaspoon ground nutmeg
¼ cup brandy

1 envelope active dry yeast
2 tablespoons lukewarm water
1 cup milk
⅓ cup shortening
¼ cup sugar
1 teaspoon salt
1 egg, beaten
4 cups all-purpose flour

Soak fruit, nuts, and spices in the brandy overnight.

Soften yeast in the lukewarm water. Scald milk, add shortening, sugar, and salt, and cool to lukewarm. Beat in egg. Empty milk mixture into mixing bowl. Stir in softened yeast and 2 cups of the flour. Beat thoroughly, then add remaining flour.

Let rise in a warm place for about 1½ hours, or until double in bulk. Turn out on floured board and knead, adding more flour if necessary to make a medium-firm dough. Let rise again for about 1½ hours, or until double in bulk.

Punch dough down and knead the fruit mixture into the dough. Divide dough in half and place each half in greased loaf pan. Let rise for about 1 hour, or until loaves are double in bulk.

Preheat oven to 400°. Brush tops of loaves with a little melted butter or milk. Bake in preheated oven for 10 minutes; reduce oven temperature to 350° and continue to bake for 50 minutes.

Cool, then frost with Thin Decorator's Frosting (see page 110), flavored with almond extract.

Makes 2 small loaves.

AUSTRIAN FILLED ROLL

4 cups all-purpose flour
1½ cups sugar
1 teaspoon salt
1 envelope active dry yeast
½ cup lukewarm milk
2 eggs, lightly beaten

4 tablespoons melted butter, cooled
  to lukewarm
½ cup honey
½ pound chopped walnuts
½ cup chopped raisins
4 squares unsweetened chocolate,
  shredded

In mixing bowl combine 3 cups flour, sugar, and salt. Soften yeast in the milk and add it, along with the eggs and melted butter, to the flour mixture.

Mix and knead, adding as much of the remaining cup of flour as necessary to make a soft smooth dough. Let rise until double in bulk, about 1½ hours, then punch down and roll out on lightly floured surface ½ inch thick; spread with honey. Sprinkle with walnuts, raisins, and chocolate. Roll up like a jelly roll and place on oiled baking sheet. Let rise until double in bulk, about 45 minutes. Bake in a 350° oven for 25 minutes, or until lightly browned. When still warm, spread with Confectioners' Sugar-Butter Glaze or Thin Decorator's Frosting (see page 110), and sprinkle with chopped walnuts.

GERMAN KUGELHOF

1 cake or envelope active dry yeast
1 cup milk, scalded then cooled to
   lukewarm
1 cup butter
¾ cup sugar
5 eggs

4 cups all-purpose flour
1 teaspoon salt
Grated rind of 1 lemon
1 cup raisins
½ cup chopped blanched almonds

Soften the yeast in the lukewarm milk. Cream the butter and sugar until light and fluffy and add the eggs, one by one, creaming well after each addition. Stir in the flour, salt, lemon rind, raisins, and half the almonds.

Butter a fancy kugelhof form or tube pan, sprinkle with the remaining almonds, and pour the batter in until the form is half full. Allow to rise in a warm place until the pan is full. Bake at 400° for 10 minutes. Reduce oven temperature to 350° and bake for another 40 minutes.

Makes 1 loaf.

Kugelhof with Chocolate: Make a kugelhof dough but omit the raisins and nuts and add enough flour to make a dough that is soft but not sticky. Divide the dough into two parts. Melt 2 ounces sweet chocolate in 3 tablespoons milk. Add 1 teaspoon vanilla and 2 tablespoons sugar. Mix this into one part of the dough. Roll out each part on a lightly floured sheet and place the chocolate mixture over the white dough. Roll up like a jelly roll and place in a well-buttered kugelhof pan or tube pan. Allow to rise until doubled in bulk and bake at 400° for 10 minutes. Lower heat to 350° and bake 45 minutes longer.

Filled Kugelhof: Make a kugelhof dough, omitting the raisins and nuts. Butter a fancy kugelhof pan generously and pour in half the batter. Sprinkle with 3 ounces ground almonds, 2 tablespoons sugar, 3 ounces chopped raisins, 1 teaspoon cinnamon, and the grated rind of 1 lemon. Pour over remaining dough and allow to rise in a warm place until the pan is full. Bake at 350° for 45 minutes. Cool on a cake rack and serve dusted with powdered sugar.

FRENCH SAVARIN

1 *cake or envelope active dry yeast*	⅔ *cup butter*
½ *cup lukewarm milk*	½ *teaspoon salt*
2 *cups all-purpose flour*	1 *tablespoon sugar*
4 *eggs, lightly beaten*	

Soften the yeast in the lukewarm milk. Sift the flour into a bowl and add the yeast mixture. Add the eggs and work all together until the dough is elastic. Work the butter until it is softened and distribute it in small quantities over the paste, mixing it in lightly. The dough should be softer than brioche dough. Cover and place in a warm spot until double in bulk. Work the dough again, adding the salt and sugar. Fill a well-buttered ring mold two-thirds full and again allow it to rise in a warm place until it almost fills the mold. Bake at 400° for about 30 minutes, or until a cake tester comes out clean.

Savarin is nice served with a macedoine of cooked fruit in the center of the ring, or served plain with apricot sauce. It may be baked in small individual ring molds, well buttered and sprinkled with toasted almond slivers, then soaked with light syrup while still warm and sprinkled with rum or kirsch.

Makes 1 loaf.

MEXICAN PAN DULCE (Sweet Egg Buns)

2 cakes or envelopes active dry
  yeast
1 tablespoon sugar
1½ cups lukewarm water
About 5 cups all-purpose flour

½ teaspoon salt
1½ cups sugar
2 tablespoons melted butter
4 eggs, beaten

Dissolve the yeast and 1 tablespoon sugar in the water. Allow to stand for 15 minutes, then stir in 2 cups of the flour and the salt. Allow to rise until double in bulk. Stir down and add 1½ cups sugar, the melted butter, eggs, and enough flour to make a dough that is soft but not sticky. Turn out on floured board and knead until dough is smooth and satiny.

Allow to rise until double in bulk, punch down, and knead again, using a little more flour if necessary. Form into small, round buns and place them, almost touching, on a greased baking sheet. Coat the tops with an icing made by mixing 1½ cups flour, 1 cup sugar, 1 beaten egg, ½ cup butter, ¼ cup heavy cream, and 1 teaspoon cinnamon to a paste. Let rise in a warm place until doubled in bulk, then bake at 350° for 30 minutes.

Makes 4 dozen buns.

CONFECTIONERS' SUGAR-BUTTER GLAZE

Mix until smooth 1½ cups confectioners' sugar, 2 tablespoons soft butter, and 3 tablespoons light cream or fruit juice. Flavor with ½ teaspoon vanilla or almond extract, or stir in 1 tablespoon grated lemon or orange rind.

THIN DECORATOR'S FROSTING

A simple frosting for sweet rolls and coffee cakes is made by adding a few tablespoons hot milk or water to 1 cup confectioners' sugar and mixing it to a spreading consistency. Flavor it with ½ teaspoon vanilla, almond, or lemon extract. The frosting should not be too thick and should be spread over the bread or rolls while warm but not hot.

GARNISH

Sweet breads and rolls can be made holiday bright and gifty-looking by garnishing them with shredded coconut, candied fruit, candied fruit peel, citron, blanched almonds, walnuts, or poppy seeds.

BRIGHT AND BEAUTIFUL COFFEE CAKES

It takes very little longer to make a large batch of sweet yeast dough than it does to make enough for a coffee cake or loaf. In one short morning you can have four different shapes and flavors of coffee cakes or rolls made and baked and cooling on racks. Once thoroughly cool, a tight wrapping of transparent film or aluminum foil readies them for the freezer, where they rest in all their splendor until the night before Christmas. Three can be gift-wrapped for neighboring friends. The fourth? You might set it out on the breakfast table for Santa to sample when he comes down the chimney to fill the stockings! He'll leave enough for *your* breakfast, I hope!

BASIC SWEET COFFEE CAKE DOUGH

3 envelopes active dry yeast or	*1 teaspoon salt*
2 yeast cakes	*1 cup butter*
½ cup lukewarm water	*10–12 cups all-purpose flour*
2 cups milk	*4 eggs, beaten*
1 cup sugar	

Soften yeast in the lukewarm water.

Scald milk; add sugar, salt, and butter and cool to lukewarm. Pour milk mixture into a mixing bowl and stir in enough of the flour to make a thick batter. Then stir in softened yeast and eggs and beat thoroughly. Add enough additional flour to make a dough that is soft but does not stick to the hands. Turn out on lightly floured surface and knead until smooth and satiny. Place dough in an oiled bowl, turn dough around so that all surfaces are oiled, cover lightly and let rise in a warm place until double in bulk, about 1½ hours. Punch dough down and let rest for 10 minutes.

This recipe makes enough dough for 4 different-flavored coffee cakes, as follows ... [Divide dough into four parts.]

SNOWBALL LOAF

Into one part of the basic coffee cake dough, knead 1 teaspoon grated lemon rind and 1 cup mixed diced candied fruits and peels. Shape into a ball, place on oiled cookie sheet, and pat the top to flatten it slightly.

Cover and let rise until almost double in bulk, about 45 minutes. Bake in a 350° oven for 25–30 minutes. While still slightly warm, frost with one of the frostings on page 110 and decorate with candied cherries and citron.

Makes 1 loaf.

FRUITED TEA RING

Roll out another part of the basic coffee cake dough on a lightly floured surface to a rectangle about 18 inches long and ¼-inch thick. Spread the dough with 2 tablespoons soft butter and sprinkle with ½ cup sugar mixed with 2 teaspoons cinnamon. Sprinkle with ½ cup mixed candied fruits and peels. Roll lengthwise as for a jelly roll and seal the long edge. Shape into a ring and place sealed-side-down on an oiled baking sheet. Seal the ends of the ring. With scissors, cut two-thirds of the way through the roll at 1½-inch intervals. Turn each section slightly to one side.

Cover and let rise until almost double, about 45 minutes. Bake in a 350° oven for 25 minutes. While slightly warm, frost with one of the frostings on page 110 and decorate.

Makes 1 ring loaf.

BUBBLE LOAF

With the third part of the dough, make this sticky bubble loaf.

Pinch off walnut-sized pieces of dough and shape into balls. Dip balls into melted butter and arrange a layer, with balls slightly separated on bottom of a buttered loaf pan. Arrange a second layer on top of first, placing the balls in the spaces between the dough balls in the first layer. Arrange a third layer in the same manner. Pour Caramel Glaze over all and let rise in a warm place until double in bulk, about 1 hour. Bake at 350° for 30–35 minutes. Let cool in pan for 5 minutes before turning out onto cake plate to cool. Chopped nuts may be sprinkled on each layer if desired.

Makes 1 loaf.

CARAMEL GLAZE:

Combine ½ cup dark corn syrup, 2 tablespoons melted butter, 1 teaspoon lemon juice, and grated rind of 1 lemon.

HOLIDAY KOLACKY

With the last part of the sweet yeast dough, make a pan of these jam-filled buns.

Divide dough into 12 pieces and form each piece into a ball. Place the balls 2 inches apart on an oiled baking sheet and let rise in a warm place for 15 minutes. Press down the center of each roll with the thumb to make a hollow, leaving a raised rim about ¼-inch thick around the outside. Brush hollows with melted butter and fill with jam or jelly. Let rise until double in bulk, about 45 minutes, then bake at 350° for 20 minutes. When cool, dust generously with confectioners' sugar.

Makes 12 rolls.

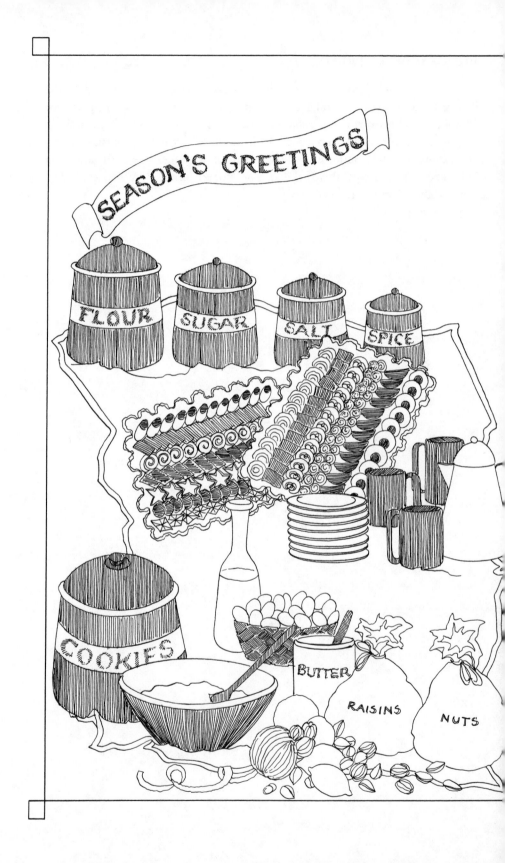

8

Around the World with Holiday Cookies

Every country of the world and every section of every country has its own special holiday cookie treats, and the ones in this chapter are especially designed for giving. They keep well, some actually improve with age, and all, except a baker's dozen of them, can be shipped safely to spread the holiday spirit across our land or from one land to another. While other gifts may be more sophisticated and more costly, few can convey a warmer greeting to neighbor or friend than a gift of cookies made in your own kitchen.

So with the fruitcakes and plum puddings soaked in brandy, wrapped in foil, and laid away to season; the quarts of spicy mincemeat lined up on a shelf in a cool room; the freezer bulging with yeasty, eggy sweet breads, it's time to lay in a fresh supply of butter, eggs, sugar, raisins, candied fruits, and nuts and turn our attention to cookie-making. Even homemakers to whom "cookie" may be a "no-no" word during most of the year can't resist baking and decorating several batches of cookies to nibble on during the merry days that precede Christmas.

The recipes are easy and fun to make, so let small hands help drop or fashion or roll out and cut the rich dough into different shapes and sizes. With a little imagination one versatile cookie dough can be turned into a dozen different types and flavors of cookies. But before giving the recipe, a few cookie-making tips.

COOKIE-MAKING TIPS AND A RECIPE
FOR BASIC COOKIE DOUGH

When making cookies, be careful not to roll in a lot of extra flour or the cookies will taste floury. Roll out a small amount of dough at a time using, if possible, a canvas pastry cloth and stockinette rolling pin cover.

For best flavor use real butter in cookies. The small additional cost is worth it and makes the difference between a homemade cookie and those from a commercial bakery.

If using cake flour, sift before measuring. All-purpose flour does not need to be sifted.

If a recipe calls for one kind of nut, change to another if it is more to your taste. Spices, too, can be changed and a favorite flavor substituted for another.

To grease baking sheets, use absorbent paper dipped in a little cooking oil. This is easier than using semihard shortenings or butter. Use the same oily paper to wipe off any crumbs from the sheet. It is not necessary to wash the baking sheet between batches.

Because ovens frequently vary in temperature, cookies should be checked a few minutes before the specified baking time is complete. Thinner cookies may have to be removed a little sooner; thicker ones may need a couple of extra baking minutes.

All cookie doughs, with the exception of drop batters, freeze well. If you prefer fresh-baked cookies for your own pleasure during the busy pre-holiday days, just wrap different kinds of cookie dough in individual packages. When needed, thaw dough at room temperature until it can be rolled or sliced, then bake as needed.

Store all cookies in tightly closed containers. Soft cookies will remain fresh and soft; crisp cookies will remain crisp.

For gift-giving, be on the lookout for brightly colored tins that you can paint or decoupage. Ginger jars make lovely cookie containers, tied with a big bow or with a sprig of holly or mistletoe attached. Large glass apothecary jars, available in many houseware stores, make handsome containers; they're a thoughtful gift, too, since they can be used long after your cookies have been enjoyed. But remember that the container need not be fancy or expensive—it's the thought that counts—and a batch of your homemade goodies on a plastic plate painted with a jolly Santa can be the best of gifts.

When packing cookies for shipment, wrap each cookie separately in transparent wrap and pack in an attractive container filled with shredded tissue paper. The container may be tin, wood, glass, ceramic, or cardboard. Pack the cookies firmly so they cannot rattle around. Gift-wrap, then wrap lengthwise with corrugated cardboard and insert into a slightly larger box. Pack empty space between the cookie container and the shipping box with shredded paper or styrofoam balls, overwrap in plain brown paper, and mark FRAGILE.

So now, armed with all the necessary cookie-making know-how and with visions of sugarplums dancing in our heads, on with the cookie merry-making.

First is a basic sugar cookie that lends itself to many innovations and imaginative touches to become your personal cookie achievement to say "Happy Holidays" with this year.

VERSATILE VANILLA COOKIES

1 cup butter (2 sticks)	*1 teaspoon cream of tartar*
1½ cups sugar	*1 teaspoon baking soda*
2 eggs	*1 cup milk*
3¾ cups all-purpose flour	*1 teaspoon vanilla*
Pinch salt	

Cream butter and sugar together until mixture is light and fluffy. Add eggs and beat well. Combine dry ingredients and stir into butter mixture alternately with the milk and vanilla.

Divide dough into four equal parts.

Leave one part plain. To the second part add 1 cup chopped nuts, chopped dates, or seedless raisins. *To the third part* add 1 6-ounce package semi-sweet chocolate pieces. *To the fourth part* add 1 teaspoon cinnamon, ½ teaspoon nutmeg, and ½ teaspoon ginger.

Drop batter from a teaspoon onto oiled baking sheet, keeping the mounds about 1 inch apart, and bake in a 375° oven for 10–12 minutes.

Makes about 8 dozen cookies.

CHERRY DROPS

Follow recipe for Versatile Vanilla Cookies but use almond extract in place of the vanilla. Stir into the dough 2 teaspoons grated lemon rind, ⅔ cup chopped cherries, 1 cup chopped nuts, and 1½ cups chopped moist coconut. Drop onto oiled baking sheet as above and bake in a 350° oven for 12–15 minutes.

COOKIES THAT NEED TIME TO RIPEN

The following handful of cookie recipes should be made at least three weeks before serving. They all keep well and ship well, and they may be frozen if desired.

SWISS LECKERLI

½ cup honey
½ cup sugar
Pinch salt
2 teaspoons each ground cloves
    and cinnamon
¼ cup each finely chopped candied
    orange, lemon peel, and citron

1 egg
1 teaspoon baking soda
2 tablespoons brandy or sherry
1 teaspoon grated lemon rind
1 cup chopped blanched almonds
2¾ cups all-purpose flour
Clear Syrup Glaze

In heavy saucepan bring honey and sugar to a boil. Stir in salt, spices, and peels. Remove from heat; add the egg and beat well.

Dissolve soda in the brandy or sherry and stir into mixture along with the lemon rind, almonds, and flour. Knead until well blended, form into a ball, and wrap in plastic film or aluminum foil. Chill for 1 hour. Cover a baking sheet with brown paper and oil the paper.

Roll dough out on a lightly floured surface into a rectangle ½-inch thick. Lift the rectangle onto the covered baking sheet and bake in a 325° oven for 30 minutes. Remove from oven and, while hot, brush with Clear Syrup Glaze. Cut into 2½ x 1-inch strips and transfer strips to a cake rack to cool. Store in tightly closed container for 4–5 weeks before serving.

Makes about 6 dozen cookies.

Clear Syrup Glaze: In small saucepan combine ½ cup sugar and ¼ cup water. Bring to a boil and boil until the syrup spins a thread when a little is allowed to run off the tines of a fork (234°).

LONDON FRUIT BARS

½ pound mixed candied fruits,
    chopped
½ pound candied pineapple,
    chopped
½ pound candied cherries, halved
2 cups seedless raisins
¾ cup port, sherry, or Madeira
1⅓ cups all-purpose flour
1 cup light brown sugar, firmly
    packed

6 tablespoons soft butter
2 eggs
1 teaspoon ground nutmeg
1 teaspoon ground cinnamon
½ teaspoon ground cloves
½ teaspoon baking soda
½ teaspoon salt
Fine granulated fruit sugar

A day in advance, combine the fruit, pour the port, sherry, or Madeira over it, and let soak overnight.

Next day, put all remaining ingredients except fruit sugar into bowl of an electric beater. Beat on low speed until well blended, scraping sides of bowl occasionally with rubber spatula. Fold in fruit mixture.

Spread batter on a well-oiled and waxed-paper-lined jelly roll pan (15½ x 10½ inches) and bake in a 350° oven for 35 minutes, or until cake tests done. Cool in pan, then cut into bars. Roll bars in fruit sugar and store in tightly covered container. Let mellow for about 3 weeks before serving.

Makes about 48 bars.

CALIFORNIA DATE-NUT PINWHEELS

4 cups all-purpose flour	1 teaspoon baking soda
2 cups light brown sugar, firmly packed	1 teaspoon double-acting baking powder
1 cup soft butter (2 sticks)	2 teaspoons vanilla extract
2 eggs	Date-Nut Filling
2 tablespoons milk	

Measure all cookie ingredients into the bowl of an electric beater. Beat on low speed just until all ingredients are mixed, then beat on medium speed for 3 minutes, scraping sides of bowl occasionally with a rubber spatula. Wrap dough in waxed paper and chill for 2 hours.

Place a sheet of waxed paper on a working surface that's been moistened with a damp cloth to keep the paper from slipping. Flour the paper lightly.

Cut dough into four equal parts. Roll out one part on the floured waxed paper into a rectangle about 9 x 12 inches. Spread with ½ cup Date-Nut Filling and roll up lengthwise, jelly roll fashion. Wrap in the waxed paper and chill until firm. Repeat with remaining dough.

Cut jelly rolls crosswise into ¼-inch slices. Place slices ½ inch apart on well-oiled baking sheets. Bake for 10 minutes, or until golden, in a 375° oven. Remove cookies immediately to wire racks to cool. When cool, store in tightly covered container. Let age for 2 weeks before serving.

Makes 14 dozen pinwheels.

Date-Nut Filling for Pinwheels:

1 10-ounce package pitted dates, finely chopped	½ cup orange juice
½ cup sugar	1 teaspoon grated orange rind
	½ cup chopped pecans or walnuts

In saucepan combine dates, sugar, orange juice, and rind. Bring to a simmer and cook for 5 minutes, or until mixture is thickened, stirring occasionally. Remove from heat and stir in nuts. Cool.

Makes 2 cups.

SPRINGERLE

For an embossed design, use a Springerle rolling pin.

4 eggs
4 cups confectioners' sugar (1
    pound)
20 drops anise oil

3¾ cups all-purpose flour
1 teaspoon baking soda
1½–2 teaspoons crushed anise
    seeds

With electric mixer, beat eggs till light. Gradually add sugar and continue beating on high speed for 15 minutes, or until light and fluffy. Add anise oil. Sift together flour and soda; blend into egg mixture on low speed. Cover bowl tightly with waxed paper or foil and let stand for about 15 minutes. Divide dough into thirds.

On lightly floured surface, roll each third into an 8-inch square, a little more than ¼ inch thick. Let stand 1 minute. Dust Springerle rolling pin lightly with flour; roll or press hard enough to make clear design. With a sharp knife, cut the cookies apart. Place on lightly floured surface; cover with a towel and let stand overnight.

Oil baking sheets and sprinkle each with anise seeds. Brush excess flour from cookies; with finger, rub undersides very lightly with cold water and place on baking sheets. Bake in slow oven (300°) about 20 minutes, till light straw color.

Let ripen in tightly covered container for a few days before eating.

Makes 6 dozen cookies.

MERINGUE COOKIES AND MACAROONS

Meringue cookies and macaroons all improve with age. Make them several weeks before Christmas.

CHOCOLATE NUT MERINGUES

2 eggs whites
⅛ teaspoon cream of tartar
½ cup sugar
½ cup chopped pecans or walnuts

½ cup shredded coconut
1 1-ounce square semi-sweet
    chocolate, grated
1 teaspoon vanilla

Beat egg whites with cream of tartar until soft peaks form. Beat in sugar, 2 tablespoons at a time, beating until sugar is dissolved after each addition. The meringue should be stiff and glossy. Fold in remaining ingredients.

Drop mixture by the teaspoonful onto brown-paper-lined baking sheets, about 1 inch apart. Bake in a 250° oven for 40 minutes. Cool cookies on racks and store in tightly covered container.

Makes 3 dozen cookies.

ITALIAN MACAROONS

1 cup blanched almonds
1¼ cups sugar
2 large egg whites, lightly beaten
½ teaspoon almond extract
9 candied cherries, halved

Dry almonds thoroughly in a warm oven for 10–15 minutes, then grind until powdery in container of an electric blender.

Mix the ground almonds with 1 cup of the sugar and gradually beat in enough of the egg whites to make a soft, thick batter. Beat thoroughly, then beat in the almond extract.

Drop by teaspoonfuls onto a baking sheet lined with plain brown paper. Sprinkle with remaining sugar and put half a cherry in center of each. Let stand for 3–4 hours at room temperature, then bake in a 375° oven for about 20 minutes, or until dry and light golden brown. Store in airtight container when thoroughly cooled.

Makes 1½ dozen macaroons.

HAZELNUT MACAROONS

2 egg whites   *1 cup ground hazelnuts*
1 cup sifted confectioners' sugar   *18 whole hazelnuts*
1 tablespoon lemon juice

Beat egg whites until foamy. Sprinkle with sugar and lemon juice and continue to beat until meringue becomes stiff and forms glossy peaks. Fold in ground nuts.

Drop by teaspoonfuls, about 1 inch apart, on baking sheet lined with plain brown paper. Place a whole nut in center of each and let stand at room temperature overnight.

Next day, bake in 350° oven for 15–20 minutes, or until golden. Makes 1½ dozen macaroons.

COCONUT ALMOND MACAROONS

¾ cup sugar
1 cup almond paste
Pinch salt
1 teaspoon vanilla

3 egg whites
1 cup shredded coconut
¾ square unsweetened chocolate, melted

Beat the sugar gradually into the almond paste. Add salt and vanilla. Then add egg whites, one at a time, beating well after each addition. Stir in coconut.

Divide mixture in half. To one half stir in the melted chocolate; leave the other half plain. Drop by teaspoonfuls on ungreased brown paper spread on baking sheets. Bake in 300° oven for 30 minutes, or until just dry on the surface. Remove from brown paper while still warm and let stand, covered, in a cool place overnight. They should be chewy in the center. Store in tightly closed container to keep them from drying out.

Makes 2 dozen macaroons.

NATIONAL AND INTERNATIONAL HOLIDAY COOKIES

From state to state and country to country, around the world we go with a treasure trove of national and international holiday cookie recipes. They all are good keepers and fine for shipping.

FINSKA PINNAR

1 cup sweet butter (2 sticks)
½ cup sugar
1 teaspoon almond extract
1½ cups all-purpose flour
2 egg yolks

2 tablespoons cold water
½ cup finely chopped blanched almonds
Sugar for sprinkling

Cream butter, then gradually add sugar and cream together until mixture is light and fluffy. Add flavoring and gently stir in flour until just blended.

Pinch off small pieces of dough and with lightly floured hands, roll dough into long strips about the thickness of a little finger and 2–3 inches long. Place on baking sheets.

Beat egg yolks with cold water. Brush the "fingers" with egg mixture and sprinkle with almonds and sugar. Bake in a 375° oven for 10 to 12 minutes, or until golden.

Makes 3 dozen cookies.

LEBKUCHEN

2 cups all-purpose flour
½ teaspoon salt
1 teaspoon baking powder
½ teaspoon ground cloves
1 teaspoon ground cinnamon
1 cup coarsely broken walnuts
1 8-ounce jar chopped mixed
   preserved fruits

3 eggs
1 egg yolk
1½ cups dark brown sugar, firmly
   packed
½ cup strong coffee or sherry
Sugar Frosting

Combine flour, salt, baking powder, cloves, cinnamon, nuts, and fruit. Beat eggs and egg yolk until thick and lemon-colored (use an electric beater for this if possible at high speed for 5 minutes). Gradually beat in sugar, then stir in flour mixture alternately with the coffee or sherry.

Spoon into an oiled 15 x 10½ x 1-inch jelly roll pan and bake in a 375° oven for 25 minutes, or until cake tester inserted in center comes out clean. Cool in pan.

When cool, frost with Sugar Frosting; before the frosting dries, mark it with a wet knife into 2 x 2½-inch bars. When dry, cut into bars.

Makes 30 bars.

SUGAR FROSTING:

Mix 1 cup confectioners' sugar with 2–3 tablespoons warm milk and ½ teaspoon favorite extract.

GERMAN ANISBLACHEN

4 eggs
1¼ cups sugar
2¾ cups all-purpose flour
1 tablespoon lightly crushed anise seeds

Beat eggs and sugar with rotary beater until mixture is very thick and pale in color. Add flour gradually, mixing well after each addition. Stir in anise seeds.

Drop from a teaspoon onto a well-oiled baking sheet, making mounds 1 inch apart. Let stand overnight at room temperature. Next day, bake in a 300° oven for about 20 minutes, or until very lightly browned.

Makes about 6 dozen cookies.

SWEDISH KONJAKSKRANSAR

2½ *sticks sweet butter*   *About 3 cups all-purpose flour*
⅔ *cup sugar*   ½ *cup sugar*
1 *egg yolk*   1 *teaspoon ground cinnamon*
3 *tablespoons bourbon or brandy*

Cream butter and sugar until mixture is light and fluffy. Beat egg yolk and bourbon or brandy; stir into butter mixture. Gradually add just enough flour to make a smooth but soft dough. Gather dough into a ball, wrap in waxed paper, and chill for 2 hours.

Work with a small amount of the dough at a time; keep rest refrigerated. Pinch off small pieces of dough and, on lightly floured board, roll each piece into thin pencil strips, each about 5 inches long. Twist together in pairs, then shape into rings, pressing the ends together. Place on oiled baking sheet and sprinkle lightly with mixture of cinnamon and sugar.

Bake at 350° for about 10 minutes, or until slightly golden. Cool and store in airtight container.

Makes 6 dozen cookies.

NEW ENGLAND SNICKERDOODLES

1 *cup sweet butter (1 stick)*   ½ *teaspoon baking soda*
¾ *cup sugar*   ½ *teaspoon ground nutmeg*
1 *whole egg*   ½ *cup coarsely chopped walnuts*
1 *egg yolk*   ½ *cup seedless raisins*
1½ *cups all-purpose flour*   *Sugar for sprinkling*

Cream together butter and sugar until light and fluffy. Beat in egg and egg yolk. Combine flour, baking soda, and nutmeg and stir into batter. Fold in nuts and raisins.

Drop from a teaspoon, 2 inches apart, onto oiled baking sheet and bake in a 375° oven for 10–12 minutes. Remove while still warm to cake rack to cool. Sprinkle with sugar and store in airtight container.

Makes 5 dozen cookies.

SWEDISH GINGER COOKIES

1 cup butter (2 sticks)
1½ cups sugar
1 egg
1½ tablespoons grated orange peel
2 tablespoons dark corn syrup
3 cups all-purpose flour

2 teaspoons baking soda
2 teaspoons cinnamon
1 teaspoon ginger
½ teaspoon cloves
Blanched almonds, halved

Thoroughly cream the butter and sugar. Add egg and beat until light and fluffy. Add orange peel, corn syrup, and water; mix well. Sift together dry ingredients; stir into creamed mixture. Chill dough thoroughly.

On lightly floured surface, roll to ⅛ inch thickness. Cut in desired shapes with floured cookie cutter. Place 1 inch apart on ungreased baking sheet. Top each cookie with blanched almond half. Bake in moderate oven (375°) for 8–10 minutes.

Makes about 8 dozen cookies.

CARACAS CHOCOLATE DROPS

1 6-ounce package semi-sweet
   chocolate pieces
½ cup butter (1 stick)
½ cup sugar
1 egg

1 cup all-purpose flour
½ teaspoon baking soda
½ teaspoon salt
¼ cup water
½ cup chopped nuts

Melt half the chocolate pieces. Blend butter, sugar, egg, and melted chocolate. Stir in combined ingredients alternately with the water. Stir in nuts and remaining chocolate pieces.

Drop batter from a teaspoon onto baking sheet and bake at 350° for 12–15 minutes.

Makes about 3 dozen drops.

BERLINER KRANSER

1 cup butter (2 sticks)
½ cup sugar
2 egg yolks
2 hard-cooked egg yolks, sieved

2¼ cups all-purpose flour
1 egg, lightly beaten
Candy decorettes

Thoroughly cream butter and sugar. Add the uncooked egg yolks, one at a time, beating well after each. Stir in sieved egg yolks. Add flour, stirring only enough to blend.

On lightly floured surface, roll small pieces of dough under your hands to pencil-size, about 5 inches long and a little over ¼-inch thick. (If dough gets sticky, flour hands lightly.) Form each in circle, bringing one end over other. For traditional Berliner kranser, make circle by bringing one end over and through in single knot. Brush with lightly beaten egg. Dip in candy decorettes. Bake on ungreased baking sheet in moderate oven (350°) about 10–12 minutes, or until set but not brown.

Makes about 3½ dozen cookies.

PORTUGUESE SUGAR BALLS

1 *cup butter, softened (2 sticks)*	2 *cups enriched flour*
¼ *cup sifted confectioners' sugar*	1 *cup chopped pecans*
2 *teaspoons vanilla*	*Red- and green-colored sugar*
1 *tablespoon water*	

Thoroughly cream butter, confectioners' sugar, and vanilla. Stir in water. Add flour and mix well. Stir in nuts. Shape into 1-inch balls and roll some in red sugar, some in green.

Bake 1 inch apart on ungreased baking sheet in slow oven (300°) for 20 minutes, or until firm to touch. Cool thoroughly before removing from pan.

Makes about 4 dozen balls.

NEW ENGLAND BLACK WALNUT BALLS

½ *cup butter*	1 *cup all-purpose flour*
½ *cup sifted confectioners' sugar*	½ *cup finely chopped black*
1 *tablespoon brandy*	*walnuts*
1 *teaspoon vanilla*	

Cream together butter and sugar until mixture is fluffy. Stir in brandy and vanilla. Stir in flour and nuts; mix well.

Shape dough into balls about ¾ inch in diameter and place on unoiled baking sheet. Bake in a 325° oven for 20 minutes, or until lightly browned. If desired, roll in additional confectioners' sugar.

Makes 3 dozen balls.

DANISH SOUR CREAM CRESCENTS

1 cup butter (2 sticks)   *½ cup apricot preserves*
1¾ cups all-purpose flour   *½ cup flaked coconut*
1 egg yolk   *½ cup finely chopped pecans*
½ cup commercial sour cream   *Sugar*

With pastry blender or two knives, cut butter and flour until mixture resembles fine crumbs. Beat egg yolk with the sour cream and blend into flour mixture with a fork. Gather dough into a ball and chill for several hours or overnight.

Divide dough into four equal portions. Work with one portion at a time, keeping rest refrigerated. Roll out onto a lightly floured surface into a circle about 10 inches in diameter. Spread with 2 tablespoons of the apricot preserves and sprinkle with 2 tablespoons of the coconut and pecans. Cut into twelve wedges and roll each wedge into a crescent beginning at the wide end and rolling to the point. Repeat with the rest of the dough, one quarter at a time.

Place on unoiled baking sheets and sprinkle with a little granulated sugar. Bake in a 350° oven for 20 minutes, or until lightly browned. Remove from baking sheet to cake racks to cool.

Makes 4 dozen crescents.

PEPPER NUTS

Black pepper is used in these popular spicy drop cookies found throughout Northern Europe at Christmastime. In Denmark they are called Pebernodder; in Sweden, Pepparnotter; and in Germany, Pfeffernusse.

2 eggs   *½ teaspoon each ground cloves,*
¾ cup dark brown sugar, firmly   *allspice, and black pepper*
*   packed*   *3 cups all-purpose flour*
¾ cup granulated sugar   *1 teaspoon baking soda*
½ teaspoon grated lemon rind   *Rum or brandy*
1 tablespoon each finely minced *Confectioners' sugar*
*   citron and candied orange peel*   *Confectioners' Sugar Frosting*
½ cup ground almonds   *(see page 110)*
1 teaspoon ground cinnamon

Beat eggs with both brown and granulated sugar until mixture is thick and light in color. Stir in lemon rind, citron, orange peel, almonds, and spices.

Combine flour and baking soda and stir into egg mixture. Turn dough out on lightly floured board and knead until smooth, working in a little more flour if necessary.

Shape into long rolls 1 inch thick; cut ½-inch slices. Place slices on oiled baking sheet and let dry at room temperature overnight. Bake at 300° for about 20 minutes. Sprinkle with rum or brandy and, while still warm, roll in confectioners' sugar, or cool and frost with Sugar Frosting.

Makes 6 dozen cookies.

CREOLE NUT SQUARES

½ cup butter (1 stick)
1 cup light brown sugar, firmly packed
2 eggs
2 cups chopped pitted dates

1 cup chopped pecans
1 teaspoon vanilla
⅔ cup all-purpose flour
1 teaspoon baking powder
Confectioners' sugar

Cream butter and sugar until light and fluffy. Beat in eggs. Stir in remaining ingredients and spread batter in an oiled 9-inch square pan. Bake in a 350° oven for 40–45 minutes. While warm, cut into squares and roll each square in confectioners' sugar.

Makes 16–20 squares.

MOROCCAN COCONUT CHEWS

½ cup butter (1 stick)
1 cup brown sugar, firmly packed
1 cup all-purpose flour
2 eggs
½ cup light corn syrup
1 teaspoon vanilla

2 tablespoons flour
1 teaspoon baking powder
½ teaspoon salt
1 cup shredded coconut
1 cup coarsely chopped nuts

Cream butter and ½ cup brown sugar. Stir in the 1 cup flour. Pat mixture onto bottom of an unoiled 9 x 9 x 2-inch pan. Bake in a 350° oven for 10 minutes.

Meanwhile, blend eggs and remaining ½ cup brown sugar. Stir in corn syrup and vanilla. Add 2 tablespoons flour, baking powder, and salt; mix well. Stir in coconut and nuts. Spread nut mixture over baked dough, return to oven, and bake for 25 minutes longer, or until golden brown.

Cool in pan, then cut into bars.

Makes 24 bars.

ENGLISH ORANGE-SPICE CHRISTMAS COOKIES

1 cup butter (2 sticks)
1 cup sugar
1 cup dark corn syrup
1 tablespoon grated orange peel
6 teaspoons ground cinnamon
1 teaspoon each ground cloves and
   cardamom

½ teaspoon salt
Dash pepper
5 cups all-purpose flour
1½ teaspoons baking soda
1½ cups finely chopped almonds

In a 3-quart saucepan combine the butter, sugar, and corn syrup. Heat, stirring, until melted and blended. Remove from heat and stir in orange peel, cinnamon, cloves, cardamom, salt, and pepper. Sift flour with soda into first mixture; mix well, using your hand to work in last of flour and the almonds. Form into rolls about 2 inches in diameter; wrap tightly and refrigerate.

Slice ⅛ inch thick and arrange on ungreased baking sheets. Bake in 350° oven for 8–10 minutes, or until light brown. Cool 5 minutes, then remove to cake racks.

Makes 8–10 dozen cookies.

For cookie cut-outs, roll dough, without chilling, on lightly floured board to ⅛ inch thick; cut with cookie cutters and bake as above.

BELGIAN CHERRY CAKES

1 cup soft butter (2 sticks)
½ cup confectioners' sugar
½ teaspoon almond extract
½ cup finely chopped nuts
2¼ cups sifted cake flour

1 pound red candied cherries
Confectioners' Sugar Frosting (see
   page 110)
Additional cherries for garnish

Cream together butter and sugar until light and fluffy. Stir in almond extract and nuts. Stir in flour, then gather dough into a ball. Wrap dough in waxed paper and chill until firm. Divide dough into four portions. Work with one part at a time, keeping rest refrigerated.

Shape each piece into a roll about 1 inch in diameter; cut the rolls into ½-inch lengths. Turn cut side up and press a cherry in the center of each. With lightly floured hands, shape each piece into a ball, completely covering the cherry with dough. Put on unoiled baking sheet and bake in a 350° oven for 15–20 minutes. Cool on cake racks.

When cool, place racks over waxed paper and spoon thin Confectioners' Sugar Frosting over the cookies, covering them completely. (Any frosting that runs off may be scraped up again and reused.) Decorate each cookie with a slice of candied cherry.

Makes about 8 dozen cookies.

TURKISH ALMOND COOKIES

⅔ cup butter	2 teaspoons baking powder
1 cup sugar	½ teaspoon salt
1 egg	3 tablespoons very strong coffee
2¾ cups all-purpose flour	½ cup chopped almonds

Cream together butter and sugar until mixture is light and fluffy. Beat in egg. Combine flour, baking powder, and salt and stir into egg mixture alternately with the coffee. Fold in almonds.

Chill dough thoroughly, then roll out thinly and cut into a variety of shapes with cookie cutters. Place cut-outs on oiled baking sheets and bake in a 375° oven for 8–10 minutes. Cool on racks.

Makes about 9 dozen small cut-outs.

OLD-FASHIONED AMERICAN SUGAR COOKIES

This is excellent for any kind of cookie cut-outs that you'd like to make. The basic recipe can be adapted to several different flavors of cookies. These can be cut with a cookie cutter but are not good for intricate patterns cut with a knife.

1 cup butter (2 sticks)	2½ cups all-purpose flour
1 cup sugar	½ teaspoon cream of tartar
1 egg	½ teaspoon baking soda
⅓ cup milk	¼ teaspoon salt
1 teaspoon vanilla	

Cream butter and sugar until mixture is light and fluffy. Add egg, milk, and vanilla and beat until blended. Gradually stir in dry ingredients. Roll out on unoiled baking sheets and bake in a 400° oven for 5–7 minutes.

Makes about 5 dozen cookies.

Spice Cookies: Add ½ teaspoon each cinnamon and nutmeg and ¼ teaspoon cloves.

Nut Cookies: Use 1½ cups brown sugar, firmly packed, in place of the granulated sugar. Add 1 cup finely chopped nuts.

Coconut Cookies: Add 1 cup shredded moist coconut in basic recipe or in place of the nuts in nut cookies.

Orange Cookies: Use orange juice in place of milk and add 2 tablespoons grated orange rind.

FRENCH YULE LOGS

2¼ cups enriched flour
½ cup confectioners' sugar
¼ teaspoon salt
¾ cup butter (1½ sticks)

½ cup molasses
1 teaspoon vanilla
1 cup chopped nuts

Blend flour, sugar, and salt. Cut in butter. Stir in molasses and vanilla until dough is smooth. Chill dough for at least 1 hour.

Break off small lumps of dough and shape into "logs" about 3 inches long. Roll in chopped nuts and arrange on ungreased baking sheet. Bake at 325° for 15 minutes.

Makes 3 dozen logs.

POLISH PECAN BARS

½ cup butter (1 stick)
¼ cup granulated sugar
3 eggs
1¼ cups all-purpose flour
Pinch salt
2 teaspoons vanilla

1½ cups brown sugar
½ cup shredded coconut
1 cup chopped pecans
2 tablespoons all-purpose flour
½ teaspoon baking powder

Cream butter with the granulated sugar and 1 egg. Stir in the 1¼ cups flour, salt, and 1 teaspoon of the vanilla. Pat into an oiled 9 x 12-inch pan and bake in a 350° oven for 15 minutes.

Combine remaining 2 eggs, the brown sugar, remaining vanilla, the coconut, pecans, the 2 tablespoons flour, and the baking powder. Spread the brown sugar mixture over the top of the baked dough and bake for 25 minutes longer.

Cool in the pan for a few minutes, then cut into bars and transfer bars to a rack to cool completely.

Makes 32 bars.

SWISS CHOCOLATE COOKIES

⅔ cup butter (1½ sticks)
1 cup sugar
1 egg
2 1-ounce squares unsweetened
  chocolate, melted
2½ cups all-purpose flour

1 teaspoon baking powder
½ teaspoon salt
¼ teaspoon cinnamon
⅓ cup milk
1 teaspoon vanilla

Soften butter and beat in sugar, egg, and chocolate. Combine dry ingredients and add alternately with milk and vanilla, mixing well after each addition.

Roll out ⅛ inch thick on lightly floured surface and cut into desired shapes. Place on oiled baking sheets and bake at 400° for 5–7 minutes.

Makes about 5 dozen cut-outs.

DAKOTA NUT TRIANGLES

1 cup soft butter (2 sticks)
1 cup light brown sugar, firmly
  packed
1 teaspoon vanilla
1 egg yolk
1¾ cups all-purpose flour

½ teaspoon salt
1 teaspoon ground cinnamon
½ cup finely chopped walnuts or
  pecans
1 whole egg, lightly beaten

Cream butter and sugar together until light and fluffy. Beat in vanilla and egg yolk. Combine flour, salt, and cinnamon and stir into the sugar mixture along with half the chopped nuts.

Spread the dough evenly in an oiled 15 x 12 x 2-inch baking pan and brush with beaten egg. Sprinkle remaining chopped nuts on top and press lightly into the dough with palm of hand.

Bake in a 350° oven for 25–30 minutes. Remove from oven, run a knife around edge of the baked dough, and cut into triangles (or squares, bars, or diamonds). Remove cut cookies to racks to cool.

Makes about 5 dozen cookies.

PARISIAN CHOCOLATE-COATED COOKIES

1 cup butter (2 sticks)
¾ cup confectioners' sugar
1 tablespoon vanilla
½ teaspoon salt
1 cup uncooked rolled oats
1¾ cups all-purpose flour

1 12-ounce package semi-sweet
  chocolate pieces (2 cups)
¼ cup milk
Chopped walnuts
Shredded coconut
Chocolate sprinkles

Cream together butter and sugar until mixture is light and fluffy. Stir in vanilla, salt, oats, and flour. With fingers, shape teaspoonfuls of dough into balls, crescents, or bars. Place on ungreased baking sheets and bake at 325° for 25–30 minutes, or until edges are lightly browned. Cool on racks.

Melt chocolate in double boiler over simmering water. Stir in milk and stir over the simmering water until mixture is smooth.

Drop cookies one by one, rounded side down, into the chocolate. Lift out with 2 forks, then dip in nuts, coconut, or sprinkles. Set on racks to dry.

Makes 4 dozen cookies.

NEW ORLEANS CHOCOLATE PECAN WAFERS

½ cup butter (1 stick)
1 cup sugar
½ teaspoon salt
1 teaspoon vanilla
2 eggs

3 1-ounce squares unsweetened
  chocolate, melted
¾ cup all-purpose flour
¾ cup chopped pecans

Cream together butter and sugar until mixture is light and fluffy. Add salt and vanilla. Add eggs, one at a time, beating well after each addition. Stir in melted chocolate, flour, and nuts; mix well.

Drop from a teaspoon onto oiled baking sheets, keeping the mounds about 2 inches apart. Flatten mounds with tines of a fork, dipping fork into cold water between cookies. Bake in a 325° oven for 10 minutes.

Makes 3–4 dozen wafers.

FRAGILE COOKIES TO DELIVER BY HAND

Never to be omitted from the list of holiday cookies are a baker's dozen American and foreign beauties that do not ship well. They make delicious but fragile gift-wrap-and-carry-in-hand cookies for nearby friends and neighbors. Lucky people!

SPRITZKUCHEN

1 cup soft butter (2 sticks)
1¼ cups confectioners' sugar
2 egg yolks
½ teaspoon almond extract
1 teaspoon vanilla

Pinch salt
2¼ cups all-purpose flour
1 egg white, lightly beaten
Colored sugars, red cinnamon
candies, or finely chopped nuts

In mixing bowl cream butter and sugar until mixture is light and fluffy. Beat in egg yolks, almond and vanilla extracts, and salt. Add flour and beat until all ingredients are blended.

Put dough into a cookie press and press out fancy shapes on oiled baking sheets. Bake at 350° for 10–12 minutes. Remove to wire racks to cool.

When cool, brush with egg white and decorate with colored sugar, cinnamon candies, or finely chopped nuts.

Makes about 6 dozen cookies.

CHOCOLATE SPRITZKUCHEN

½ cup butter (1 stick)
1 cup sugar
1 egg
1 tablespoon milk

1¾ cups all-purpose flour
Pinch salt
2 1-ounce squares unsweetened
chocolate, melted and cooled

Blend butter and sugar, beat in egg, and stir in milk alternately with the flour. Stir in salt and chocolate.

Fill a cookie press half full and press out cookies on unoiled baking sheet. Bake in a 375° oven for 8–10 minutes.

Makes about 5 dozen cookies.

FRENCH LACE COOKIES

1 cup all-purpose flour
1 cup finely chopped walnuts or
    pecans
½ cup corn syrup

½ cup butter (1 stick)
⅔ cup light brown sugar, firmly
    packed

Combine flour and nuts. Put corn syrup, butter, and brown sugar in top of a double boiler and bring to a boil over direct heat. Remove from heat; stir in flour and nuts.

Drop batter from tip of a teaspoon onto baking sheet covered with aluminum foil, keeping the mounds 3 inches apart and baking only 6 cookies at a time. (Keep the batter over simmering water to keep it warm between batches.) Bake in a 325° oven for 8–10 minutes. Remove from oven and let stand for 1 minute, or until crisp. While still quite warm, gently pull each cookie away from the foil and place on cake rack to cool completely.

Makes 2 dozen cookies.

BRANDY SNAP CURLS

½ cup molasses
½ cup soft butter (1 stick)
1¼ cups sifted cake flour
1 teaspoon salt

⅔ cup sugar
1 tablespoon ground ginger
3 tablespoons brandy

In saucepan heat molasses to simmering. Add butter and stir until butter is melted. Remove from heat and stir in flour, salt, sugar, ginger, and brandy.

Drop by half-teaspoonfuls onto oiled baking sheet about 3 inches apart, making six at a time. Bake in a 300° oven for about 10 minutes. Remove from oven, cool 1 minute, then remove with spatula and immediately roll around the handle of a wooden spoon. If removed too soon, wafer will crush and crinkle; if not soon enough, it will be too brittle to roll. If too brittle, return to oven for a few minutes to soften.

Repeat until all of mixture is used, lightly oiling baking sheet each time with a paper towel and removing any crumbs at the same time.

Makes about 7 dozen curls.

BUTTER PECAN ROLL-UPS

6 *tablespoons butter*	½ *teaspoon vanilla*
1 *cup brown sugar*	6 *tablespoons all-purpose flour*
1 *egg*	1 *cup finely chopped pecans*
Pinch salt	

Cream together butter and sugar. Add egg and beat until well blended. Stir in salt, vanilla, flour, and nuts.

Drop 6 teaspoonfuls, a teaspoon at a time, on oiled baking sheet, keeping the drops 3 inches apart. Bake in a 350° oven for 7 minutes. Remove from oven, let cool for a few seconds, then loosen with a spatula and curl each drop around the handle of a wooden spoon while still soft enough to roll.

Makes 8 dozen roll-ups.

Work with 2 baking sheets at a time. One can be baking while you are rolling the one that just came out of the oven.

WALNUT CRESCENTS

1 *cup butter (2 sticks)*	1 *cup chopped walnuts*
½ *cup confectioners' sugar*	1¾ *cups all-purpose flour*
2 *teaspoons vanilla*	*Confectioners' sugar for topping*
Pinch salt	

Cream butter with sugar until mixture is light and fluffy. Add vanilla and salt; beat well. Stir in nuts and flour. Gather dough into a ball, wrap in waxed paper, and chill until firm.

Divide dough into eight equal parts. On lightly floured work surface shape each part into a thin roll about ½ inch in diameter. Cut the rolls into 2-inch lengths, taper the ends, and curve into crescents.

Put crescents on unoiled baking sheets and bake in a 300° oven for 18–20 minutes. Remove to rack to cool. When cool, sift confectioners' sugar over tops and store in airtight container.

Makes 5 dozen crescents.

LITTLE BUTTER ROSETTES

½ cup soft butter (1 stick)
⅓ cup sugar
3 egg yolks
2 tablespoons milk

Pinch salt
1¾ cups all-purpose flour
Slivered almonds or candied
    cherries, quartered

Cream together butter and sugar. Add egg yolks and beat thoroughly. Stir in milk, salt, and flour.

Fill cookie press and press out rosettes about 1½ inches in diameter on oiled baking sheets. Insert a slivered almond or a quarter of a cherry in center of each rosette.

Bake in a 350° oven for 12–15 minutes. Remove to racks to cool.

Makes about 3 dozen rosettes.

Before baking, the dough may be brushed with egg white beaten with 1 tablespoon water, and sprinkled with finely chopped nuts mixed with 1 tablespoon sugar.

CHOCOLATE-VANILLA PINWHEELS

1¼ cups all-purpose flour
¼ teaspoon baking powder
Pinch salt
½ cup butter
½ cup sugar

1 egg
1 teaspoon vanilla
1 1-ounce square unsweetened
    chocolate, melted and cooled

Combine flour, baking powder, and salt. In mixing bowl blend butter and sugar thoroughly. Beat in egg. Stir in flour mixture and vanilla and divide dough in half.

To one half add the chocolate and mix into dough. Wrap both halves in plastic or waxed paper and chill until firm enough to roll, about 2 hours.

Roll out chocolate dough thinly on lightly floured board into a rectangle. Roll out vanilla dough to same size and thickness and place on top of the chocolate rectangle. Trim edges and roll lengthwise like a jelly roll. Wrap in waxed paper again and chill overnight or for several hours.

Slice crosswise ¼ inch thick. Place slices cut side down on oiled baking sheet and bake in a 350° oven for 9–10 minutes.

Makes about 4 dozen pinwheels.

COCOA AND VANILLA COOKIES

1 cup butter (2 sticks)	*½ teaspoon salt*
¼ cup sugar	*2 teaspoons vanilla*
2¼ cups all-purpose flour	*2 tablespoons cocoa*

Blend butter and sugar thoroughly. Stir in flour, salt, and vanilla; divide dough in half. To one half work in the cocoa.

Shape dough into two rolls about 1 inch in diameter and cut each roll in half crosswise. Place one chocolate and one vanilla roll close together on waxed paper. Place second vanilla roll on top of chocolate roll, and second chocolate roll on top of vanilla. Press firmly together, wrap in waxed paper, and chill for several hours. Slice crosswise about ¼ inch thick, place slices, cut side down, on oiled baking sheet, and bake at 350° for 8–10 minutes.

Makes 4 dozen cookies.

BORDERED COOKIES: To make these, two cutters of the same shape, one slightly smaller than the other, are necessary. With larger cutter, cut a cookie from each shade of dough. With smaller cutter, cut center from each cookie. Transfer the center of the vanilla dough to the center of the chocolate dough and transfer the center of the chocolate dough to the center of the vanilla dough, thus making two bordered cookies. Chill before baking.

STRIPED AND CHECKERBOARD COOKIES: To make checkerboard cookies, you first make striped cookies. Roll out light and dark dough about ¼ inch thick. Cut four oblongs of identical size from each dough. Stack oblongs one atop the other, alternating colors. Press stack together firmly. Wrap the stack in waxed paper and chill.

For checkerboards: Before chilling striped dough, slice the dough crosswise ¼ inch thick. Stack eight slices, one atop the other, turning every other slice so that a dark stripe rests on a light stripe. Press firmly together, wrap tightly in waxed paper, and chill.

When ready to bake, cut striped or checkerboard dough across stripes or checks into ¼-inch slices. [Lift slices carefully with spatula to oiled baking sheets and bake at 350° for 8–10 minutes.]

ALMOND GINGER COOKIES

1 cup butter (2 sticks)	2 teaspoons cloves
1 cup sugar	1 teaspoon baking soda
½ cup molasses	1 teaspoon salt
1 tablespoon ginger	1 cup chopped blanched almonds
2 teaspoons cinnamon	3¼ cups all-purpose flour

Blend butter and sugar. Stir in molasses, spices, soda, salt, almonds, and flour. Turn onto floured board and knead until dough is smooth. Shape into thick rolls or oblongs, wrap in waxed paper, and chill.

Cut crosswise into ¼-inch slices, place on oiled baking sheet, and bake at 350° for 8–10 minutes.

Makes 8 dozen cookies.

HUNGARIAN CHOCOLATE SQUARES

1 1-ounce square unsweetened chocolate	¼ cup all-purpose flour Pinch salt
¼ cup butter (½ stick)	½ teaspoon vanilla
½ cup sugar	½ cup finely chopped walnuts or
1 egg	pecans

Put chocolate and butter in small saucepan and heat over low heat, stirring constantly, until melted and blended. Do not overheat. Remove from heat and stir in sugar, egg, flour, salt, and vanilla.

Spread the mixture in an oiled 13 x 9 x 2-inch baking pan and sprinkle with the nuts. Bake in a 400° oven for about 12 minutes. Cool slightly; cut into 1-inch squares while still very warm. When cold, remove from pan to cake racks.

Makes 4 dozen squares.

GREEK KOURABIEDES

1 cup butter (2 sticks)	1 teaspoon cloves
2 cups confectioners' sugar	⅛ teaspoon salt
2 egg yolks	2 cups ground blanched almonds
2 cups flour	Candied fruit for decoration
1 teaspoon cinnamon	

Cream butter and sugar; add egg yolks and beat well. Sift flour, spices, and salt together; add ground almonds. Mix flour mixture with butter mixture; shape into 1-inch balls.

Place on oiled baking sheets and bake at 350° for about 15 minutes, or until golden brown. Cool on rack. When cool, roll in confectioners' sugar.

Makes about 4 dozen cookies.

And last but not least, Scotch shortbread, without which my Christmas, at least, would not be complete.

SCOTCH SHORTBREAD

20 tablespoons fine granulated sugar
5 cups all-purpose flour
1 pound sweet butter

Sift flour and sugar together three times and set aside.

Gradually work flour-sugar mixture into butter with fingers until it is the consistency of cornmeal. Press together into a ball, turn out on floured board, and knead thoroughly, adding a little more flour if necessary, until the dough begins to crack.

Roll out ⅜ inch thick and prick the dough all over with the tines of a fork. Cut into small shapes and place on oiled baking sheets. Bake in a preheated 325° oven for 20–25 minutes, or until very lightly browned. Do not overbake. The cookies should be pale in color.

Makes 54 small rounds.

9

"C" is for Christmas, Children, and Holiday Confections

It is Christmas Day that inspires the months of planning, the weeks of baking, the days of shopping; it is the children who inspire the candy-making and sugarplum concoctions that bring back so many shared memories and family traditions and add new dimensions to your family's Christmas, this year and for many years to come. Christmas, children, and candy are a trio as impossible to separate as the stripes on a candy cane.

In many health-and-tooth-conscious homes, candy may be forbidden fruit during most of the year, but on Christmas all caution is thrown to the wind as everyone from tots to teens to grandma and grandpa gorge themselves on the sweet delights that mom made.

Candy is the frosting on the cake, it is the part of Christmas remembered long after the tinsel is faded and the toys outgrown. It is the tender memory of those magical confections, all rich and sticky, those happy moments when taffy was pulled into honey-colored strands with buttered hands, that remain a part of Christmas never to be forgotten by the young and young-at-heart.

Not for the young in years, however, is the creating of nougats, nut brittles, caramels, and fondants. At this stage of the candy-making, children should be kept as far away as possible from the boiling syrups with their temperatures soaring to 300°. It is only when the time comes to shatter the peanut brittle, cut and wrap the creamy fudge, or pull the lukewarm syrup into ropes that young and willing fingers come to the aid of the candy cook.

Sugar, molasses, honey, corn syrup, nuts, candied fruits, and flavored extracts are the essential ingredients in candy-making, while the most important utensils are a heavy saucepan and a candy thermometer to measure the temperature of the syrup. When sugar and water are cooked together, the water gradually evaporates as the syrup becomes more concentrated; and the more concentrated the syrup, the hotter it gets. At first it spins a fine thread when a little is allowed to run off the tines of a fork (234°), and as the temperature increases, the syrup goes through various stages known as soft ball, firm ball, hard ball, light crack, hard crack, and finally caramelization.

The approximate temperature of the syrup can be determined by what is known as the "cold water" test, but the precise moment when the syrup must be removed from the heat is ticklish, and a candy thermometer is ever so much more dependable and accurate.

COLD WATER TEST

Use a fresh cup of cold water for each test. Pour about ½ teaspoon of the syrup into the cold water. Pick the syrup up in the fingers if possible and roll it into a ball.

Soft Ball: The syrup will roll into a soft ball that quickly loses its shape when removed from the water.

Firm Ball: The candy will roll into a firm but not hard ball and will flatten out a few minutes after being removed from the water.

Hard Ball: The syrup will roll into a hard ball which has little or no plasticity and will roll around on a plate when removed from the water.

Light Crack: The syrup will form brittle threads that will become soft when removed from the water.

Hard Crack: The syrup will shatter into brittle threads that will remain brittle when removed from the water.

Caramelization: The syrup becomes a golden brown, and if allowed to remain on the heat will become dark gold and finally a burnt brown—and a ruined saucepan. If golden caramel is desired, the pan should be set into shallow water to prevent further cooking.

The following chart shows the relationship between temperatures on a candy thermometer and the various stages of the cold water test.

TYPE OF CANDY	CANDY THERMOMETER	COLD WATER TEST
Fondant, fudge	234–238°	Soft ball
Divinity, caramels	245–262°	Firm ball
Taffy	265–270°	Hard ball
Butterscotch	275–280°	Light crack
Peanut brittle	285–300°	Hard crack
Caramelized sugar	310–320°	Golden brown to dark gold

Candy is fun to make, and most of it is quite easy providing a few basic candy-making rules are followed.

Choose a good day. Don't make candy on warm humid days, especially hard taffies and nut brittles. They will absorb moisture from the air and become sticky.

Use a heavy-bottomed saucepan. It should be four times as large as the volume of ingredients. Syrups boil up in pans and can boil over before you have time to say "Happy Holiday" if the saucepan is too small. What a mess it can make of your stove!

Follow recipes exactly. Never double ingredients in a candy recipe. Better to make two batches.

Never cool candy in the refrigerator. The cold air in the refrigerator is moist air and can spell disaster for candy.

Use best ingredients. Pure butter and fresh rich cream are going to give you super candy. Evaporated or condensed milk are generally used only in fudges.

Cut candy with a firm-bladed knife—one that does not bend. Mark the line of cutting, then cut with a back-and-forth sawing motion.

SO-EASY CANDIES FOR CHILDREN TO HELP MAKE

Before getting down to the real nitty-gritty of Christmas candy-making, let's bring the children into the kitchen to help us with some sugarplum sweet-meats and other simple but delicious candies that are safe for little hands to help make. They—the candy, not the children—may be prettily boxed and safely shipped by air or parcel post.

SUGARPLUMS

Many different combinations of dried fruits may be used to make those visions that dance in children's heads come true. They keep best in the refrigerator and ripen in several weeks.

Put dried fruits through the fine blade of a meat grinder along with some walnuts and candied fruit peels and cherries. You can use apricots, peaches, figs, prunes, apples, or pears. Moisten the dried fruits with enough fruit juice, dark rum, or good brandy to bind all together. Shape into small plums and roll in granulated sugar several times as the mixture of fruit and liquid absorbs the sugar. Let dry for an hour or so on waxed paper, then store in a waxed-paper-lined tin with tight cover and put in the refrigerator to ripen.

Tiny bags of sugarplums make an unusual treat when Christmas carolers come a-calling.

STUFFED DATES

5 prunes	1 teaspoon vanilla
5 figs	1 teaspoon honey
⅓ cup pecan meats	34 pitted dates
⅓ cup seedless raisins	Fine fruit sugar
½ teaspoon cinnamon	

Wash the prunes and figs and steam them for 10 minutes. Remove pits from prunes and put through coarse blade of a food chopper with the figs, nuts, and raisins.

Combine the fruit mixture with the cinnamon, vanilla, and honey. Stuff the dates with the fruit mixture and roll in sugar.

Makes 34 stuffed dates.

APRICOT COCONUT BALLS

1 cup dried apricots	1 tablespoon lemon juice
1 cup flaked coconut	1 tablespoon orange juice
¾ cup chopped nuts	Confectioners' sugar
1 teaspoon grated lemon rind	

Put apricots, coconut, and nuts through fine blade of a food grinder. Knead ground mixture with lemon rind, and lemon and orange juice. Add enough confectioners' sugar to make a firm mixture. Form into small balls and roll in confectioners' sugar. Let dry at room temperature for at least 4 hours.

Makes about 1 pound.

SUGARED NUTS

2 teaspoons soft butter	1 cup sugar
1 pound mixed nut meats	Pinch salt
¼ cup butter (½ stick)	⅓ teaspoon cinnamon
2 egg whites	

Butter a shallow baking pan with the 2 teaspoons butter, sprinkle nuts on top and bake in a 325° oven for 20 minutes, stirring frequently. Cool.

In shallow jelly roll pan melt the ¼ cup butter. Beat egg whites until they form moist peaks. Combine sugar, salt, and cinnamon and gradually beat into the egg whites. Beat until egg whites are stiff and glossy. Fold in nuts.

Spread nut mixture over melted butter and bake at 325° for 40 minutes. Cool and break into chunks. Store in tightly covered container.

Makes 1 pound.

CHOCOLATE NUT MOUNDS

Very quick, very easy, and very rich.

1 1-ounce square unsweetened chocolate	2 cups chopped walnuts
⅔ cup sweetened condensed milk (6-ounce can)	1½ teaspoons vanilla

Melt chocolate over hot water. When smooth, stir in condensed milk and mix well. Stir in walnuts and vanilla.

Drop by scant teaspoonfuls onto buttered baking sheet and bake in a 350° oven about 15 minutes.

Makes 4 dozen mounds.

COCOA BALLS

½ cup cocoa	1 teaspoon vanilla
1 cup chopped nuts	1 tablespoon cocoa
1½ cups confectioners' sugar	2 tablespoons confectioners' sugar
½ cup sweetened condensed milk	

Combine the ½ cup of cocoa with the nuts and 1½ cups sugar. Add milk and vanilla and mix thoroughly. Form into little balls and place on waxed paper to dry for half an hour.

Then combine 1 tablespoon cocoa and the 2 tablespoons sugar. Roll the balls in the cocoa mixture and store in tightly closed container.

Makes 2 dozen balls.

QUICK NUT FUDGE

1 pound confectioners' sugar
½ cup cocoa
¼ teaspoon salt
6 tablespoons butter

4 tablespoons milk
1 tablespoon vanilla
1 cup chopped nuts

Combine all ingredients except nuts in top of double boiler. Place over hot water and stir until smooth. Add nuts and mix. Spread in 9 x 5-inch buttered pan. Cool and cut in squares, then wrap.

Makes 2 dozen 1-inch pieces.

NO-COOK CHOCOLATE FUDGE

4 1-ounce squares sweetened
  chocolate
2 tablespoons melted butter
1 pound confectioners' sugar

3 tablespoons strong coffee or milk
1 tablespoon vanilla
Nuts (optional)

Melt butter and chocolate together over low heat, stirring until smooth. Combine sugar and coffee or milk; stir until mixture is as smooth as silk. Stir in melted chocolate and vanilla; add nuts if desired.

Makes 1½ pounds.

CHOCOLATE TRUFFLES

1 12-ounce package semi-sweet chocolate pieces
Dash salt
⅔ cup sweetened condensed milk (6-ounces)
1 teaspoon vanilla

Melt chocolate over hot water. Remove from heat and stir in salt and condensed milk. Beat with a fork until mixture is smooth and well blended. Stir in flavoring.

Pour into oiled 7 x 3 x 2-inch loaf pan and chill for 24 hours. Cut into pieces; wrap each piece in waxed paper and store in tightly covered container.

Makes 1⅓ pounds.

COBBLESTONE CANDY

2 12-ounce packages butterscotch pieces
2 tablespoons butter
3 cups miniature marshmallows
2 cups coarsely chopped walnuts

In top of double boiler combine butterscotch pieces and butter over hot, but not boiling, water, stirring occasionally. When mixture is smooth, remove from heat and stir in marshmallows and nuts.

Spread mixture in a foil-lined 13 x 9-inch baking dish and chill for about 3 hours, or until firm. Remove from refrigerator, let stand at room temperature for a few minutes, then cut into squares.

Makes about 120 squares.

DUTCH CHRISTMAS BALLS

1 cup sugar
Grated rind of 2 oranges
2 tablespoons orange juice

1 teaspoon lemon juice
1 cup finely chopped candied fruit
Dutch cocoa

In saucepan melt sugar with orange rind, orange juice, and lemon juice over low heat. Cool; add candied fruit and work with hands until well mixed.

Pinch off bits of the mixture, roll into balls, and roll balls in sifted cocoa.

Makes about 16 balls.

CARAMEL CHEWS

36 vanilla caramels
3 tablespoons light cream
1 cup cornflakes

1 cup crispy rice cereal
1 cup flaked or shredded coconut
1 cup chopped pecans

Melt caramels with cream over simmering water, stirring occasionally. Toss together cereals, coconut, and nuts. Pour caramel mixture over. With buttered mixing spoon, mix thoroughly. Drop from teaspoon onto waxed paper.

Makes about 2 dozen chews.

BUTTER CREAMS

1 pound confectioners' sugar	1 teaspoon vanilla
1/4 pound butter (1 stick)	1 1-ounce square unsweetened
2 tablespoons cream	chocolate
Dash salt	

Work all ingredients but chocolate together until blended. Refrigerate for 24 hours. Mold into small balls and dip in melted chocolate. Put on waxed paper to dry.

Makes 1⅔ pounds.

SNOWBALLS

1 cup chopped dates	1½ cups confectioners' sugar
1 cup finely chopped walnuts	2–4 tablespoons light cream
1 cup peanut butter	2 ounces flaked coconut

Combine dates, walnuts, and peanut butter. Shape into small balls about 1 inch in diameter. Make a thin icing with the sugar and cream. Roll balls in the icing and then in coconut. Let stand until icing is set. May be served immediately or stored in tightly closed container.

Makes 24–30 snowballs.

SPINNING A FINE THREAD

Working our way up the candy thermometer, we begin by cooking syrup to the fine-thread stage and making lovely seafoam patties, candied fruit peels, and nuts. All keep well, and the candied fruit and nuts are good for long-distance gift-giving. They ship well if packaged in containers with tight-fitting covers. Tuck in a sprig of artificial holly for a festive touch.

SEAFOAM CANDY

3 cups brown sugar	1/2 teaspoon vanilla
1 cup water	1 cup broken nuts
2 egg whites	Pinch salt

In saucepan combine sugar and water and cook, stirring, until sugar is completely dissolved, then boil rapidly until syrup spins a long thread when a little is dropped off the tines of a fork.

Beat egg whites until stiff and very gradually beat in the syrup. Use an electric beater for this if possible, and when all syrup is added continue to beat until cool and creamy. Add vanilla, nuts, and salt. Mix and drop in patties on waxed paper.

Makes 3 dozen patties.

CANDIED FRUIT PEEL

Candied fruit peel makes an unusual holiday gift. It may be made at least a month in advance, and takes well to traveling.

2 medium oranges	*½ cup light corn syrup*
2 large lemons	*1½ cups water*
1 medium grapefruit	*1 3-ounce package lemon-flavored*
Sugar	*gelatin*

With a sharp knife cut the peel from the fruit. (Use the fruit for breakfast fruit cup.) Cut the peel into long thin strips. Put peel into a large kettle containing 8 cups boiling water and boil for 15 minutes. Drain peel in colander, rinse, and repeat with 8 cups fresh hot water.

In large saucepan combine sugar, corn syrup, and 1½ cups water. Bring to a boil, stirring constantly, until sugar is dissolved. Stir in well-drained peels, reduce heat, and cook slowly for about 40 minutes, or until fruit has absorbed most of the syrup. Stir occasionally.

Remove peel from heat and stir in gelatin. Cool for 10 minutes.

Coat a sheet of waxed paper heavily with about 1 cup sugar. Lightly roll peels in the sugar, a few at a time, adding more sugar if needed. Arrange sugar-coated peels in single layer on wire racks and let dry overnight. Store in tightly covered container.

Makes about 8 cups.

CANDIED APRICOT FINGERS

1 12-ounce package dried apricots
1 medium orange
2½ cups sugar

Wash and drain apricots. Wash orange and cut in quarters, peel and all. Finely grind the apricots and orange. Place in 2-quart saucepan. Add 1½ cups sugar; blend and bring to boil. Boil for 8 minutes over low heat, stirring constantly. Cool slightly. Drop by spoonfuls into remaining 1 cup sugar.

Roll into fingers about 2 inches long. Dry thoroughly and store in airtight container.

Makes about 2 pounds.

CREAMY, LUSCIOUS FUDGE FOR THE HOLIDAYS

Fudge is as American as the Fourth of July, and as easy to make as shooting off a firecracker. For gift-giving, or shipping, pour the beaten fudge directly into shallow gift boxes lined with waxed paper, and after it sets, mark it into squares or cut through without removing the squares from the box. This keeps the fudge from drying out. If you prefer to package individual pieces, each square should be wrapped in waxed paper or transparent film before it is packaged, then overwrapped for gift-giving.

For best results, use a candy thermometer in making fudges.

BLONDE FUDGE

2 tablespoons butter	*1 cup light cream*
3 cups sugar	*½ cup milk*
¼ cup light corn syrup	*2 teaspoons vanilla*
Pinch salt	*1 cup coarsely chopped nuts*

In a saucepan combine butter, sugar, corn syrup, salt, cream, and milk. Bring to a boil over medium heat, stirring constantly. Continue cooking, stirring occasionally, until a small amount forms a soft ball when dropped into very cold water (234°). Remove from heat. Add vanilla and cook to lukewarm (110°).

Beat syrup until the fudge begins to thicken and loses its gloss. Fold in the nuts. Spread into a buttered, foil-lined 8-inch square pan. When cold, lift out with the foil and cut into squares.

Makes 1½ pounds.

MAPLE CREAMS

1½ cups pure maple syrup
½ cup heavy cream
Pinch salt
Pecan halves or blanched almonds

In a heavy saucepan combine syrup, cream, and salt. Bring to a boil, stirring until well blended, then cook until a little dropped into cold water forms a soft ball (236°). Do not stir while it is boiling. Pour syrup onto a platter and let stand until lukewarm (110°). Then heat the syrup until it becomes light in color and begins to set. Roll a teaspoonful at a time in palms of the hands and place on buttered baking sheet. Press a pecan or almond into each round, flattening it slightly.

Makes ⅔ pound.

CHOCOLATE HONEY FUDGE

2 cups sugar	1 cup evaporated milk
1 1-ounce square unsweetened chocolate	¼ cup honey
	2 tablespoons butter
¼ teaspoon salt	1 cup nuts

Boil sugar, chocolate, salt, and milk for 5 minutes, stirring until sugar is completely dissolved. Add honey and cook to soft-ball stage (236°). Add butter; let stand until lukewarm.

Beat until creamy; add nuts and pour into buttered pan. Cut into squares when firm.

Makes 2 pounds.

CHRISTMAS FUDGE

3 cups sugar	1½ teaspoons vanilla
¼ teaspoon cream of tartar	½ cup chopped nuts
¼ teaspoon salt	¼ cup chopped dates
1 cup light cream	¼ cup chopped candied cherries
1 tablespoon butter	

In heavy saucepan combine sugar, cream of tartar, salt, and cream. Heat, stirring, until sugar is dissolved. Bring to a boil and wipe down sides of pan with a moistened pastry brush or piece of cloth wrapped around the tines of a fork. Boil without stirring to the soft-ball stage (236°).

Remove from heat, drop in butter, cool without stirring to 110°. Add vanilla and beat until mixture loses its gloss and holds its shape. Stir in nuts and fruit and pour into buttered 12 x 8-inch pan. Cool, then cut into squares.

Makes 96 1-inch squares.

RAISIN-NUT FUDGE CLUSTERS

½ cup evaporated milk	*¼ cup butter (½ stick)*
½ cup water	*1 teaspoon vanilla*
½ teaspoon salt	*1 cup nuts*
2 cups sugar	*1 cup seedless raisins*

Combine milk, water, salt, and sugar and cook to soft-ball stage (236°).
Put butter in a heavy skillet and heat to a light brown; add to sugar mixture.
Do not stir until cooled. Add vanilla and beat until creamy. Add nuts and
raisins and drop from spoon onto waxed paper.

Makes 2 pounds.

WHOLESOME HOLIDAY CARAMELS

Caramels are a Christmas favorite, and when properly made will stay tender
and chewy for at least two weeks. If they are not dipped into melted chocolate,
they must be wrapped in waxed paper or transparent film to prevent them
from becoming either too soft or too hard. Package them in boxes or other
tightly closed containers; overwrap for gift-giving with transparent film and
tie with a big red bow. Anyone receiving a gift of homemade caramel candies
is a lucky person and will be blessed with love and good fortune during the
entire New Year.

Divinities, light-airy sweetmeats, are generally formed into small individual patties. They may, however, be cooked in pans and, like caramels,
cut into squares and individually wrapped. They will remain moist for at
least a week if stored in a tightly closed container.

CARAMELS

2 cups sugar	*¾ cup evaporated milk*
1⅓ cups light corn syrup	*¼ cup butter (½ stick)*
2 cups heavy cream	*2 teaspoons vanilla*
Pinch salt	*2 cups broken pecans (optional)*

In heavy saucepan combine sugar, corn syrup, 1 cup of the cream, and salt.
Bring to a boil, stirring occasionally. Gradually add the remaining cream and
evaporated milk very slowly so that the mixture never stops boiling. Cook
to 240° on candy thermometer. Add butter and continue to cook, stirring
gently and constantly, until a little of the mixture dropped into cold water
forms a firm ball (246°).

Remove from heat and stir in vanilla and the pecans, if desired. Pour into a buttered 9-inch square pan and cool. When cool, turn out on board and cut into squares.

Makes about 2 pounds.

OLD-FASHIONED BLACK WALNUT CARAMELS

4 4-ounce squares unsweetened
    chocolate, grated
1 stick butter (½ cup)
1 pound light brown sugar

½ cup molasses
1 cup light cream
1 teaspoon vanilla
1 pound black walnut meats

In heavy saucepan combine chocolate, butter, sugar, molasses, and cream. Cook, stirring constantly, until sugar is completely dissolved, then cook to the firm-ball stage (246°), stirring occasionally.

Remove from heat and stir in vanilla and nuts. Mix well and pour into buttered pan. Mark into squares; when cool, cut into squares and wrap each in waxed paper.

Makes 3 pounds.

HONEY CARAMELS

1⅓ cups light cream
2 cups sugar
¼ cup butter (½ stick)

1 cup honey
1 teaspoon vanilla
1 cup nut meats

In heavy saucepan combine cream, sugar, butter, and honey. Bring to a boil, stirring constantly, then cook to the firm-ball stage (246°), stirring constantly near the end of the cooking time to prevent sticking. Remove from heat and stir in vanilla and nuts. Pour into buttered pan and cool. Cut into squares and wrap.

Makes 2½ pounds.

DIVINITY DROPS

2⅓ cups granulated sugar
½ cup light corn syrup
½ cup water
Pinch salt
2 egg whites

1 teaspoon vanilla
¾ cup brown sugar
1⅓ cups granulated sugar
1¼ cups evaporated milk
⅛ teaspoon baking soda

In heavy saucepan combine the 2½ cups sugar, corn syrup, water, and salt. Cook to the firm-ball stage (246°), stirring only until sugar is dissolved.

Meanwhile, beat egg whites to stiff peaks. Gradually pour the hot syrup into the egg whites, beating constantly at high speed with an electric mixer. Add vanilla and continue to beat until mixture is thick and cool.

With buttered hands, shape candy into ¾-inch balls. Let stand on waxed paper until dry and firm.

Meanwhile, in another heavy saucepan blend brown sugar, the 1⅓ cups granulated sugar, 1 cup of the evaporated milk, and the soda. Cook, stirring, over medium heat until mixture comes to a boil and sugar is dissolved. Boil, stirring frequently, to the soft-ball stage (230°). Remove from heat. Cool to 110° without stirring, then beat until mixture is thick and creamy and loses its gloss. Beat in remaining ¼ cup evaporated milk. If caramel becomes too stiff, add additional evaporated milk, a teaspoon at a time.

Drop the candy balls, one at a time, into the caramel, turn with a fork to coat all sides, and place on waxed paper to cool.

Makes 6 dozen drops.

TAFFIES AND NUT BRITTLES

This is fun stuff to make at any time of the year, but especially during the holiday season. It's hard to remember a Christmas without a large bowl of peanut brittle on the festive table, and every child in the world looks forward to a taffy-pull.

Taffies must be cooked to the soft-crack stage, or to 265–270°; the brittles climb close to the 300° mark.

All of the nut brittles make a fine candy for gift-giving and stand up well to shipping. They remain fresh-tasting for many weeks providing they are kept from moist air by storing them in tightly covered containers.

PULLED TAFFY

2 cups molasses
2 cups light brown sugar, firmly
* packed*
3 tablespoons butter

2 tablespoons cider vinegar
1 teaspoon vanilla
¼ teaspoon baking soda

In large saucepan combine molasses, sugar, butter, and vinegar. Bring to a boil, stirring, until all sugar is dissolved, then boil to the hard-ball stage (270°). Remove from heat and add vanilla and baking soda.

Pour the hot syrup onto a buttered platter to cool to lukewarm (110°).

When cool enough to handle, butter your hands and begin to pull a small section of the syrup at a time into a long strand, loop both ends to the middle and pull again; pull and loop until it becomes light and taffy-colored. Twist into a rope and snip with kitchen scissors into 1-inch pieces. Everyone will be well-buttered and covered with stickiness, but who cares—it's the happy holiday season.

Makes 2 pounds.

BLACK WALNUT MOLASSES TAFFY

1½ cups granulated sugar	*4 tablespoons butter*
½ cup molasses	*⅛ teaspoon salt*
1½ cups water	*¼ teaspoon baking soda*
2 tablespoons vinegar	*1 cup finely chopped nuts*
½ teaspoon cream of tartar	

Boil the sugar, molasses, water, vinegar, and cream of tartar to 270°. Add the butter, salt, and soda and pour into greased pan. When cool enough to handle, pull until light in color. Add the nuts and work them into the taffy by kneading and pulling. Pull into strips the desired thickness and cut into pieces about 1-inch long with scissors. Wrap in waxed paper.

Makes 1½ pounds.

SALTWATER TAFFY

2 cups sugar	*2 tablespoons butter*
1½ cups water	*¼ teaspoon oil of peppermint*
1 cup light corn syrup	*3 drops red or green food coloring*
1 teaspoon salt	

In saucepan combine sugar, water, syrup, and salt. Cook over medium heat, stirring constantly, until sugar is dissolved. Then continue to boil to the hard-ball stage (270°) without stirring, about 1 hour. Remove from heat and stir in butter, flavoring, and food color.

Pour into a buttered 12½ x 10½ x 1-inch pan. Cool until comfortable to handle. Butter hands lightly. Gather small amounts of the taffy into a ball and pull until the candy becomes opaque and holds its shape. Pull each piece into a long strand about ½ inch thick and cut into bite-sized pieces with buttered kitchen shears.

Wrap in waxed paper or clear plastic wrap.

Makes 1¼ pounds.

HOLIDAY LOLLIPOPS

2 *cups sugar*	*¾ teaspoon flavoring (your choice)*
⅔ cup corn syrup	*Food coloring*
1 *cup water*	*Lollipop sticks*

Put sugar, corn syrup, and water in saucepan. Stir until sugar dissolves. Cover with tight-fitting lid for a few minutes, until it comes to a boil. Remove lid and boil until syrup forms a very hard ball when dropped into water (270°); remove from heat. Add the desired flavoring and coloring.

Quickly drop from tablespoon onto well-greased pan. Insert sticks and add any desired decoration.

Makes 2 dozen lollypops.

Great for birthday treats, too!

ALMOND BRITTLE

½ cup light corn syrup	3 *tablespoons butter*
2 *cups sugar*	1 *cup halved blanched almonds*
⅓ cup water	1 *teaspoon vanilla*
¼ teaspoon salt	

In saucepan combine corn syrup, sugar, water, salt, and butter. Cook over low heat, stirring constantly, until sugar is dissolved. Stir in nuts and continue cooking over moderate heat, stirring frequently, to the hard-crack stage (300°) or when a small amount dropped into cold water breaks into brittle threads. Remove from heat and stir in vanilla.

Line a baking sheet with aluminum foil and oil the foil. Pour the candy onto the baking sheet to cool. When cool, break into irregular pieces.

Makes 1⅓ pounds.

PEANUT BRITTLE

1 *cup sugar*	2 *tablespoons soft butter*
½ cup light corn syrup	1 *teaspoon vanilla*
¼ cup water	1 *teaspoon baking soda*
1 *cup shelled peanuts*	

In heavy saucepan combine sugar, corn syrup, and ¼ cup water. Bring to a boil and boil until sugar is dissolved and syrup is clear, stirring constantly.

Stir in peanuts and continue to cook until a small amount of the syrup dropped in cold water separates into brittle threads (300°). Remove from heat and quickly stir in butter, vanilla, and baking soda.

Immediately pour onto greased cookie sheets in thin layers. When cool, break with hands into small pieces.

Store in tightly covered container.

Makes 1 pound.

BUTTERSCOTCH

2 cups sugar
2/3 cup light corn syrup
1/4 cup water

1/4 cup light cream or half and half
1/4 cup butter

Put all ingredients except butter into a saucepan and bring to a boil over medium heat, stirring constantly. Then continue to cook until a hard ball forms when a small amount is tested in very cold water (260°). Add butter and continue cooking until a small amount tested in very cold water separates into threads which are hard but not brittle (290°).

Pour into buttered 8-inch square pan. When almost set, cut into squares. When cold, break apart.

Makes 1¼ pounds, or 60 squares.

TOFFEE CRUNCH

1½ cups butter (3 sticks)
1¾ cups sugar
1/3 cup light corn syrup
1½ cups chopped walnuts or
*   blanched almonds*

4 ounces semi-sweet chocolate
*   pieces*
1/3 cup finely chopped walnuts or
*   toasted almonds*

In 2-quart saucepan melt butter. Add sugar and cook over low heat, stirring constantly, until sugar is completely dissolved. Stir in corn syrup and cook over low heat, without stirring, to 300° on a candy thermometer. Remove from heat. Stir in nuts; do not overmix.

Pour immediately into an ungreased 13 x 9 x 2-inch pan. Melt chocolate until soft and smooth and spread over the cooled toffee. Sprinkle with the finely chopped nuts. Break into irregular pieces.

Makes about 2 pounds.

ALMOND BUTTER CRUNCH

3 sticks butter (1½ cups)
2 cups sugar
1 cup sliced almonds
1 6-ounce package chocolate pieces

Cook butter and sugar over low heat until syrup reaches 260°. Add almonds and cook until syrup reaches 310° or the hard-crack stage.

Pour onto a buttered cookie sheet and let cool. Melt chocolate pieces and spread on both sides of the butter crunch. Break into pieces when cool.

Makes 2⅓ pounds.

10

Make It an Old-Fashioned Christmas

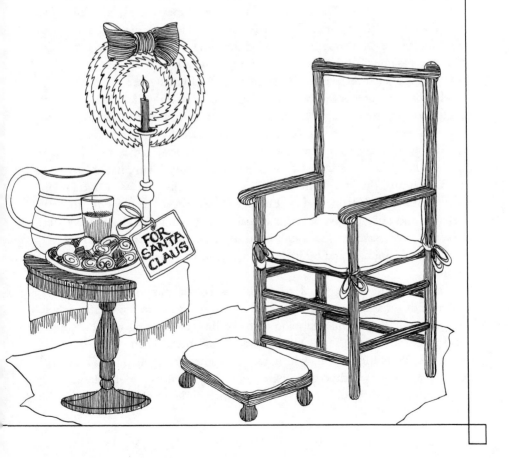

No matter how things change in this troubled world, the basic beauty of the Christmas season remains the same. It is the season of symbols, season of the best will to all men, season of peace to the whole wide world. It is a season that comes only once a year, yet there is no time throughout the year that is longer remembered.

It is a time of legends and family traditions, of special memories garnered from Christmases past. Those lovely tender, sometimes foolish moments that come flooding back: the table set for Santa with his own plate of cookies to help him on his busy way, the bulging stockings hanging from the mantlepiece, the pajama-clad procession wending its way into the living room, the squeals of delight at the ever-exciting beauty of the lighted tree.

Decorations are as much a part of Christmas as the gifts, the carols, the crisply browned turkey, or the tree itself, and there is a special joy in making your own—the giant popcorn balls, the freshly baked cookie decorations that say "Happy Holidays" all through the house—a special satisfaction is a real old-fashioned Christmas with all the touches that only loving hands can give.

Decorating the tree with cookies is a delightful Old World tradition. Since the days of Martin Luther, Europeans have baked cookies in all sorts of shapes and sizes to give a touch of gaiety and humor to the holiday tree. In Belgium, for example, the dough is baked in the form of angels; in Moravia, in the form of animals and birds; in Germany, in the form of stars and "little" people.

There should be a ritual to Christmas cookie-making, evenings, days, or weekends set aside to design and bake them. It should be fun for the whole family, especially the children, who enjoy rolling and cutting out the gingerbread men, the hearts, the stars, the reindeer, and bells. Then comes the most fun of all, decorating them, which can be endlessly fascinating. There will be sugar frosting to outline the cookie forms, tiny bright stars of colored icing pushed from a pastry tube to light up a cookiemobile, candy sprinkles for the cat's tail, candied cherries for Hansel and Gretel's noses, and sweet "glue" to cement together the sides and roof of the gingerbread house.

The how-tos are here, including some cookie patterns. Trace them same-size, or enlarge them by means of a photostat, pantograph, or graph paper and then transfer them onto cardboard. Cut the patterns out with kitchen scissors. Place the cardboard cut-outs on one of the cookie doughs recommended for cut-out cookies and cut around the cardboard patterns with a sharp pointed knife. Transfer the cut-outs to an oiled baking sheet with a wide spatula or pancake turner, keeping the cut-outs at least 1 inch apart. Bake according to the recipe until lightly browned. Let cool for a few minutes before either moving them to cake racks or pushing them to another spot on the baking sheet to make sure they will not stick.

The cookie patterns herein are but a small sampling of the possibilities. Many others may be culled from children's coloring books, Christmas and gift cards, from picture books of birds and animals. In size they can range from one-biteful or tree-ornament size to those large enough for a wall decoration, a mantlepiece decoration, or a table centerpiece. They can be simple or complex, amusing or exceptionally beautiful in design and execution. They can be as imaginative as you want them to be, an expression of your creativity and love.

COOKIE DOUGHS FOR COOKIE CUT-OUTS

First, some cookie doughs especially designed to roll out smoothly and hold their shape during baking so that the designs and figures will not be distorted.

VANILLA SUGAR COOKIE CUT-OUTS

½ cup butter (1 stick)	1 teaspoon vanilla
1 cup sugar	2 cups all-purpose flour
1 egg	1 teaspoon baking powder
⅓ cup milk	¼ teaspoon salt

Blend butter, sugar, egg, milk, and vanilla until mixture is smooth. Gradually stir in combined dry ingredients.

Roll out on floured board ⅛ inch thick and cut into desired shapes. Transfer to oiled baking sheets and bake in a 375° oven for about 8 minutes.

Makes 5 dozen small cookies.

Sugar Spice: Omit vanilla and add ½ teaspoon nutmeg and 1 teaspoon cinnamon to the dry ingredients.

Butterscotch: Use 1½ cups light brown sugar in place of the granulated sugar.

Orange: Add 2 tablespoons grated orange rind and use orange juice in place of the milk.

CHOCOLATE COOKIE CUT-OUTS

⅔ cup butter
1 cup sugar
1 egg
2 1-ounce squares unsweetened
    chocolate, melted
2⅓ cups all-purpose flour

1 teaspoon baking powder
½ teaspoon salt
¼ teaspoon cinnamon (optional)
⅓ cup milk
1 teaspoon vanilla

Blend butter, sugar, egg, and chocolate. Stir in combined dry ingredients alternately with the milk and vanilla. Add a little additional flour if needed to make a soft but not sticky dough.

Roll out on floured surface ⅛ inch thick and cut into desired shapes. Place on oiled baking sheets and bake at 375° for about 8 minutes.

Makes 6 dozen small cookies.

SNAPPY GINGER COOKIE CUT-OUTS

⅔ cup sugar
½ cup butter (1 stick)
⅔ cup molasses
1 egg
1 teaspoon ginger

1 teaspoon cinnamon
½ teaspoon cloves
2½ cups all-purpose flour
1 teaspoon baking soda

Combine sugar, butter, molasses, and egg. Stir in spices mixed with flour and baking soda. Knead dough until smooth and roll out on lightly floured surface ⅛ inch thick.

Cut into a variety of shapes with fancy cookie cutters or cardboard cut-outs. Transfer to oiled baking sheets and bake in a 375° oven for about 8 minutes. Cool cookies on cake racks and decorate as desired.

Makes 5 dozen small cookies.

THIN MOLASSES COOKIE CUT-OUTS

1 cup soft butter (2 sticks)
1 cup light brown sugar, firmly
* packed*
1½ cups molasses
1 teaspoon vinegar
4 cups all-purpose flour

¼ teaspoon each baking soda and
* salt*
1 teaspoon ground cinnamon
½ teaspoon each ground cloves,
* nutmeg, and ginger*

A day in advance, cream butter and sugar until light and fluffy, using a large bowl. Stir vinegar into molasses and stir into the sugar mixture.

Combine flour, soda, salt, and spices and stir gradually into the sugar mixture to make a soft but not sticky dough. Knead lightly with floured hands, gather dough into a ball, wrap in waxed paper, and chill overnight.

Next day, work with a small portion of the dough at a time, keeping the rest chilled. Roll out on lightly floured surface ⅛ inch thick and cut with floured cookie cutters or cardboard patterns into a variety of shapes. Place cut-outs on oiled baking sheets and bake in a 375° oven for about 8 minutes, or until lightly browned. Cool on cake racks. Decorate with colored sugar or candies or with decorator's icing. Store in tightly closed containers.

Makes about 8 dozen cookies.

HONEY SPICE COOKIE CUT-OUTS

1 cup butter (2 sticks)
1 cup sugar
1 egg
½ cup corn syrup
½ cup honey
2 tablespoons vinegar

2 teaspoons ground ginger
1 teaspoon each ground cinnamon
* and cloves*
Dash salt
About 4 cups all-purpose flour
1 teaspoon baking soda

Cream together butter and sugar. Beat in egg, corn syrup, honey, vinegar, spices, and salt. Beat in 2 cups of the flour, then the soda. Stir in enough remaining flour to make a soft but not sticky dough. Wrap dough in waxed paper and chill for at least 3 hours.

Roll out small portions of the dough at a time about ⅛ inch thick on lightly floured surface; cut into different shapes. Transfer to an oiled baking sheet and bake in a 375° oven for 8 minutes. Cool a little, then remove to cake racks to cool.

Makes about 8 dozen cookies or a gingerbread sleigh and a cookiemobile.

Half of this amount of cookie dough will make a crèche and all its figures.

TREE ORNAMENTS FROM COOKIE DOUGH

Especially appealing to children is a Christmas tree decorated with cookies. Better plan to have a few extra tucked away to replace those that are bound to disappear each day.

Make one of the roll-out cookie doughs ⅛ inch thick and cut into the shapes of stars, crescents, candy canes, bells, and balls (see pages 168–170) for some ideas to get you started). Before baking, make a hole in the top of each ornament with a sharp instrument, keeping the hole at least ¼ inch from the top edge of the dough.

Bake and cool.

Decorate with tinted decorator's icing and silver shot or sugar crystals and cinnamon red-hots. Insert string or wire through the holes in top of cookies. Hang many on your own tree and package them by the dozen in boxes or baskets for friends and neighbors to hang on their trees.

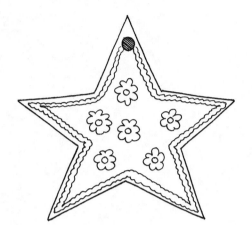

DECORATING COOKIES WITH A PASTRY BAG AND ICING

Children are fascinated with pastry bag decorating, and most will spend many happy hours pressing colored icing onto cookie cut-outs with small, unsteady hands.

You will need a couple of canvas bags and some small plain and fluted tubes. For a start, I recommend No. 3 small round tube and No. 16 small fluted tube. With these you can make straight or fluted lines, ruffled edges, stars, dots, and other fantasy designs. You will also need some bottles of food coloring and a good quantity of decorator's icing.

DECORATOR'S ICING

Blend 1 pound confectioners' sugar (sift if lumpy), ½ teaspoon salt, and 1 teaspoon vanilla with enough milk or water to make a smooth paste that will hold its shape without running. Divide into small bowls and tint each portion with a drop or two of a different food color.

Put one of the metal tubes into the pointed end of a pastry bag, put a couple of tablespoons of the icing well down into the narrow part of the bag and fold over the top several times, forcing the icing down into the pastry tube.

For Straight Lines: Hold the tube almost parallel and close to the surface of the cookie. Press out icing while drawing the tube slowly in the direction in which the line is to flow.

For Dots or Stars: Hold the tube upright, directly over the spot where the dot or star is to appear. Press gently. The harder the press, the larger the dot or star will be.

For a variety of effects on cookie cut-outs, use a combination of colored icing, halved candied cherries, and bits of candied citron or fruit rinds.

"PAINTING" COOKIE CUT-OUTS

Cookie cut-outs may be "painted" with pastel or very vivid colors *before they are baked* with a special cookie "paint" made with egg yolk and food colors.

COOKIE PAINT

Use 1 egg yolk for each different color that you plan to use. Beat 2 or 3 drops of food color into the egg yolk—easy does it, those food colors are potent. Don't plan on blue because no matter how you mix it, when you add blue food color to yellow egg yolk you get green! However, green, red, and yellow are more Christmasy colors than blue, and if you want purple, use a drop each of red and blue. For outlining cookies to give them dimension, make a brown color by beating 1 drop each of blue, green and red colors into the egg yolk.

To paint the cookies, roll out cookie dough on floured surface or between two pieces of waxed paper to ⅛ inch thickness. If using waxed paper, moisten the surface on which you are working to keep the paper from slipping.

Cut out different shapes and figures by tracing or enlarging the patterns in this book, or make your own patterns as whimsical or artistic as you please. Trim away excess dough, gather into a ball, and return to the refrigerator while painting the cookies.

Using small artists' paint brushes, first outline the cookie and any patterned design within the cookie with the dark brown, then paint in the various colors.

Transfer cookies to an oiled baking sheet and bake according to cookie recipe instructions. Let cool and, if desired, add further decorations for an embossed effect with decorator's icing and a pastry bag.

SPECIAL EFFECTS FOR HOLIDAY COOKIES

Special—or relief—effects on cookie cut-outs of people and animals are easily achieved by using currants or raisins for the eyes, half a candied cherry or a cinnamon candy for the nose, strips of candied orange peel for the mouth, and so on. These may be pressed into the dough before the cookies are baked or "glued" on after baking. Just be sure, if you use a special effect ingredient (such as chocolate bits) before baking, that it won't melt.

More time-consuming but equally effective are double cut-outs of specific parts of the design superimposed on the dough. You might, for instance, superimpose the scales on a fish, the wings on a bird, the cap and collar on a clown. "Paste" the second cut-out on top of the one outlined on the cookie cut-out with a little beaten egg white and bake as directed.

The sky's the limit so have fun! It's all up to you, your patience, and your imagination. If you combine the before-baking "painting" technique with after-baking pastry tube decorating and give a few final embellishments with candied shot, red-hots, cherries, fruit peels, and chocolate drops, there is no limit to the number of different artistic and creative effects that can be achieved.

Just in case some of you are getting discouraged at this point, here are a couple of easy gift-cookie suggestions.

MERRY CHRISTMAS GINGERBREAD

Prepare one of the three spice doughs on pages 166–167 and cut in small rounds or hearts. Use decorator's icing as "glue" and paste the cookies onto a ribbon to spell out a holiday message to your next-door neighbor—one letter of the greeting on each cookie—made of decorator's icing pressed out of a pastry tube. Fourteen cookies will give you MERRY CHRISTMAS, thirteen spells HAPPY HOLIDAYS, and nine make the abbreviated but still effective MERRY XMAS. Hang one on your mantle, too.

CANDY CANE COOKIES

1 cup soft butter (2 sticks)	Dash salt
1 cup confectioners' sugar	½ teaspoon red food coloring
1 egg	½ cup granulated sugar
1½ teaspoons almond extract	½ cup crushed peppermint candy
2½ cups all-purpose flour	

Cream butter and sugar until mixture is light and fluffy. Beat in egg and the extract. Stir in flour and salt. Divide dough in half; into one half knead the red food coloring.

Roll doughs out thinly on lightly floured surface and cut each into strips about ½-inch wide and 4 inches long. Place one strip of plain dough beside a strip of red dough and press them together where they meet. Then twist like a rope and place on unoiled baking sheets. Curve the top of each cookie down to form the handle of the cane.

Bake in a 350° oven for 9–10 minutes, or until lightly browned. Remove with spatula while still warm to cake racks to cool and sprinkle with the granulated sugar mixed with the peppermint candy.

Makes 4 dozen cookies.

THREE-DIMENSIONAL COOKIE STARS AND OTHER COOKIE FIGURES

Stars have been symbolic of Christmas ever since Martin Luther tried to tell his wife and children of the beauty of the woods shimmering in a brilliant starlit winter sky. One Christmas Eve he brought home a small fir tree, its branches alight with candles, symbolizing the forest and its starshine.

This is one of the many legends of how the Christmas tree came to be, and there is everlasting enchantment in the topmost star that hangs upon it.

The star may be rhinestone-studded or fashioned of gleaming tinsel. It may be a simple cardboard star, crayon-outlined with the uncertain hand of youth, or it might be the most old-fashioned star of all—a cookie star.

Cookie star patterns are easily cut from cardboard. Make the star cookies in a variety of sizes to hang on the Christmas tree or for a centerpiece or mantle display. Make two cut-outs of each size star. Then, following the diagram below, cut a slot about ¼ inch wide in each piece of dough, starting at the tip of a point in one and the base of a point in the other. Bake the cookies and cool. When cool, put two together as in the diagram and decorate with ruffles of colored decorator's icing.

Almost any simple pattern may be made three-dimensional by cutting and baking two of each. Before making, cut a slot ¼-inch wide through to the center of the cookie, but in opposite directions in each pair.

For a three-dimensional angel, the slot in one cookie would be from the halo to the center and the slot in the second cookie would be from the skirt to the center (see below). Bake and cool and insert one slot into the other.

For a three-dimensional bird, follow the pattern for the bird in flight shown on page 179, including the slot from tail to center of the body for the wings. After baking and decorating, slip the wings into the slot in the bird.

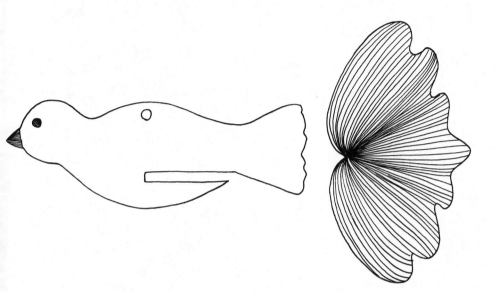

COOKIE STAR TREES

Make cookie stars in graduated sizes out of one of the recommended doughs for roll-out cookies. Before baking, cut a hole in the middle the size of a wooden dowel or a long slim pencil. Cut out some simple cookie rings too. Bake and cool. When cool, thread the stars onto wooden dowels or pencils beginning with the largest and ending with the smallest, with a ring in between each star to give separation to the "branches" of the trees. Leave them plain and arrange three on some evergreen sprigs or holly branches, or drip thin decorator's icing down them to simulate a pine tree heavily laden with snow and place them on a mirrored tray.

If you want to make the trees into candlelights, put the stars and rings together over a tall thin candle instead of the wooden dowel or pencil. Naturally, as the candles burn down, the cookies will have to be eaten, to the great delight of the small fry around the holiday table.

COOKIEMOBILES

Cookie cut-outs of various shapes and sizes may be strung into cookie-mobiles to dangle from chandelier or mantle. All the edible parts, packaged together with instructions for assembling, make a real "fun" gift for neighboring children. Let them put it together, watch it twist and twirl for a few days—then eat it!

Because we are, at the moment, talking about holiday decor, we chose for one of our cookiemobiles stars and musical angels dangling from comets, and Santa himself for another. No way need these mobiles be limited to Christmas; use hearts and arrows for Valentine's Day; chickens, ducks, and rabbits hanging from large decorated eggs for Easter; hobgoblins, witches, and pumpkins for Halloween, and so on.

Enlarge the pattern pieces to any size you wish, transfer to cardboard, and cut out the different parts from a rolled cookie dough with a sharp knife. Transfer carefully to oiled baking sheets, using a large pancake turner to lift the cut-outs. For the larger pieces, you may have to use two pancake turners, one in each hand. With a sharp instrument make holes in the parts as indicated in the pattern. Bake according to recipe directions and cool on the sheets—but while still warm, shift them from one spot to another on the sheet with a spatula to make sure they are not going to stick.

When cool, assemble the different parts according to the illustrations by tying them together with nylon thread or catgut.

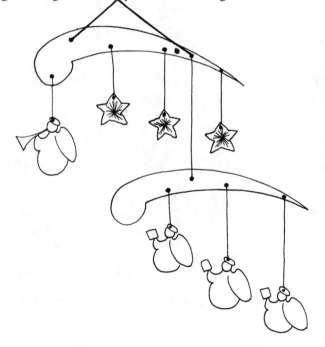

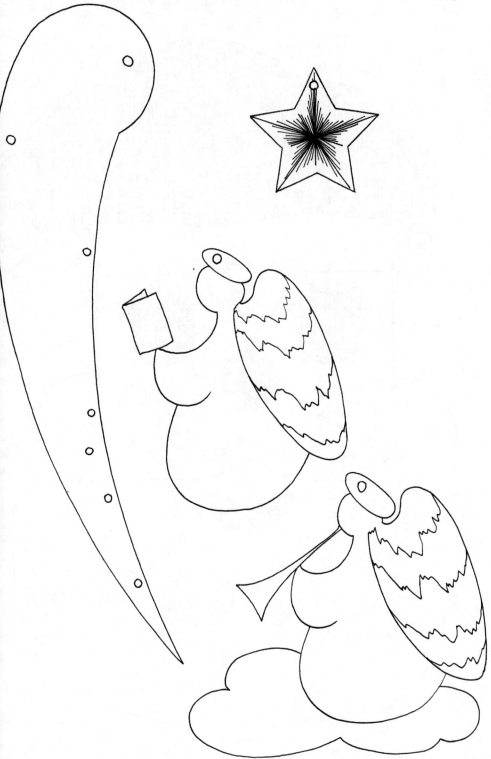

SANTA CLAUS GIFT CARD

Cut him out of cardboard to any size you want, cut him out of a rolled-out cookie dough; bake him, decorate him, and use him as a table place card or snuggle him into a basket of cookies before it is gift-wrapped. Pipe on the name of a person or a greeting with decorator's icing pressed through a pastry bag fitted with a small plain tube.

To use Santa as a table place card, he should be inserted into a baked cookie base to make him stand.

To Make Cookie Cut-Outs Stand: Almost any cookie can be made to stand upright with an edible cookie base. Cut rectangles out of cookie dough at least 1 inch wide and cut a slot about ¼ inch wide from one of the short sides of the rectangle, about three-quarters of the way through (see below). Be sure the cookie pattern you want to make stand has a "foot" on it. If it doesn't, add it when you cut the pattern out of the cookie dough. Bake the rectangles and when cool, put a dab of decorator's icing in the slot and insert the "foot" of the tree or angel or whatever else it is you wish to make stand into the slot. If necessary, use a plastic toothpick to give support to the figure until the icing has a chance to set.

You will have to use your sense of balance to make the cookie bases in proportion to the height of the cookie figures. Unless you are making your cut-outs of unusual thickness, the slots in the rectangles will remain the same—about ¼ inch.

To make Santa stand, add another ¼ inch to both his legs and after baking, insert legs into slots in rectangle of baked cookie dough along with a dab of icing.

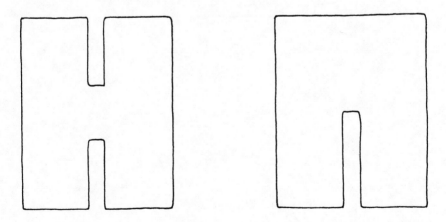

A COOKIE SLED

Any one of the recommended roll-out cookie doughs can be used to make more ambitious ornaments than tree decorations and cookiemobiles. Charming little houses and sleds can be cut from cardboard patterns and assembled with decorator's icing to hold the sections together. Use them for mantelpiece or table decorations, or place them under the tree.

The sled can be made by using the patterns shown on page 189—simply note the dimensions and trace (cut) the patterns directly onto the dough using a ruler and knife. Make a cookie base for it if you wish, or use corrugated cardboard covered with aluminum foil.

After the cookie parts are baked and cooled, decorate them with curlicues and ruffles and stars of decorator's icing before assembling. Let the icing set overnight, then glue the sides to the back and front, coating all edges that will be touching with thick decorator's icing. Insert toothpicks (the plastic ones have sharper points) from one part through to another for support, then let dry thoroughly for a few hours. Remove the toothpicks when the icing is well set. Surround the sled with pine branches or holly sprays, and fill it with cookies or with a Santa and goodie bag made from the patterns on page 190. Make several of the reindeer, arrange them on cookie stands, make reins from Christmas ribbon, and let them pull Santa's sled. These patterns won't need to be enlarged if you've followed the dimensions given for the sled itself. If you decide to put Santa on top of the sled instead of inside it, you may need to use toothpicks or an extra dab of icing to keep him upright.

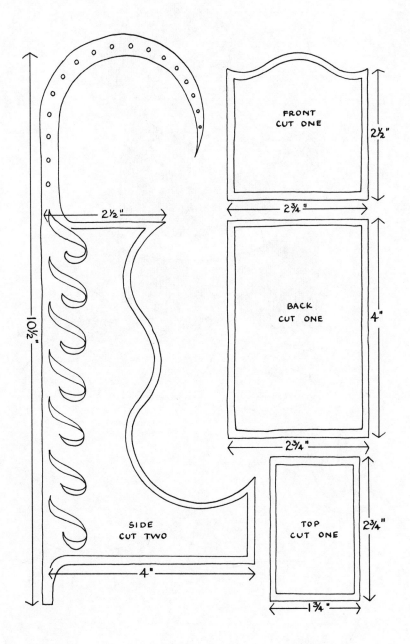

A COOKIE CRÈCHE

Another charming Christmas decoration for mantlepiece or table is a cookie crèche. It combines all the cookie techniques described in this chapter, and it can truly be a work of art, as exquisite as a stained glass window. But like any work of art, it requires time and patience. A few spare hours on several consecutive days will accomplish more and give better results than trying to rush your masterpiece through in one day. It is *not* difficult, just time-consuming, but time well spent.

The patterns for the little figures (pages 195–196) are shown actual size to fit into a manger of the size given in the diagrams on page 194. They can be increased if you wish providing the dimensions of the manger are increased proportionately.

Cut the figures out of thin cardboard or stiff paper. Make one of the roll-out cookie doughs (I used the recipe for Honey Spice Cookies). Roll out a small portion of the dough at a time, keeping the rest wrapped in waxed paper in the refrigerator. Place the figures and any of the atmosphere patterns on the dough and cut around them with a sharp knife. While the patterns are still in place, use a pin to prick the pattern into the dough at intervals along design lines within the figures. These will be your guidelines for painting and decorating the figures.

Make egg "paint," using one egg yolk for each color. You will need brown, red, green, orange, yellow, and purple. Using small artists' paint brushes, first outline the figures with brown, then paint in the various colors of the robes on the figures. Use vivid colors on the three wise men, softer peasant colors on Mary and Joseph. The infant's crib should be brown as well as the camel and, perhaps, Joseph's robe. Use royal purple on the camel's saddle, yellow for the straw, the halo around the infant, the star, and the moon, too, if you plan to use it. Leave the clouds plain but paint the trees green with brown trunks. You may use more than one camel and many trees if you wish, but if so you must plan to make room for them by enlarging the floor base of the barn to accommodate them or provide cookie bases for them.

Bake the cookie cut-outs according to recipe directions, watching carefully so that they are not overbrowned. Remove the baked cookies after a few minutes to cake racks to cool.

Roll out more dough ⅛-inch thick and, using a ruler and sharp knife, cut out the floor base, sides, roof, and back of the manger. Lift the pieces carefully onto oiled baking sheets with a wide spatula or pancake turner and square up the corners and the sides of the dough with the side of the ruler. Make indentations on the floor base where the different figures will be placed. The infant, Mary, and Joseph will be set under the roof of the manger; the wise men, the tree, the sheep, and a camel will stand just outside the manger on the floor base that represents the floor of the barn. Cut the roof in half along the dotted line in the diagram but leave the pieces together to bake.

Bake and cool on the baking sheets, but while still warm slip a spatula gently under each part and move it slightly on the sheet so that it won't stick. At this point the cookies will still be soft, so this is the time to cut slots in the floor base where the figures will be inserted and separate the roof into two parts.

Let the cookies cool and crisp.

Mix a good quantity of decorator's icing. It must be thick enough not to run or drip. Spread the frosting on the bottom and both sides of the two side pieces of the manger and place them on the floor base as indicated by the dotted lines on the diagram. Prop the walls with toothpicks to keep them upright and let dry for about half an hour, or until the "glue" is set. In similar fashion "glue" the back of the manger on the back edge of the floor and against the two sides. Prop and let dry.

To put on the roof, spread the top edges of the sides and back of the manger and the center cut of the roof with icing and set them in place. The roof will balance quite nicely on the cookie frame of the manger, but if necessary use toothpicks in strategic places to hold it in place. Remove the toothpicks when the icing is dry.

Thin remaining decorator's icing with a drop of milk to make it the right consistency to flow through a pastry tube, tint it with food coloring, and press it through a pastry bag to make pattern details on the figures. Spread white icing on the cloud. Let the icing dry before assembling the crèche.

To assemble the crèche, put a dab of icing in the slots in the manger floor and floor of the barn and insert the painted and decorated figures in the slots. Suspend the angel, star, moon, and clouds over the crèche on nylon thread.

If placing the crèche on the mantle you might like to place a dark blue felt or posterboard background behind it.

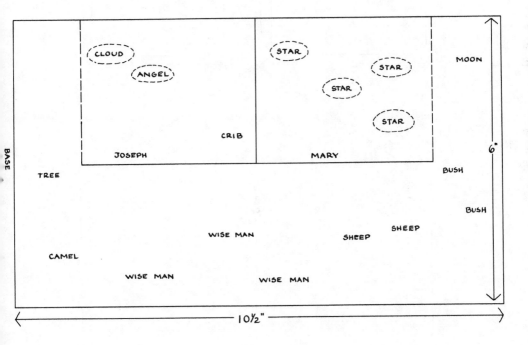

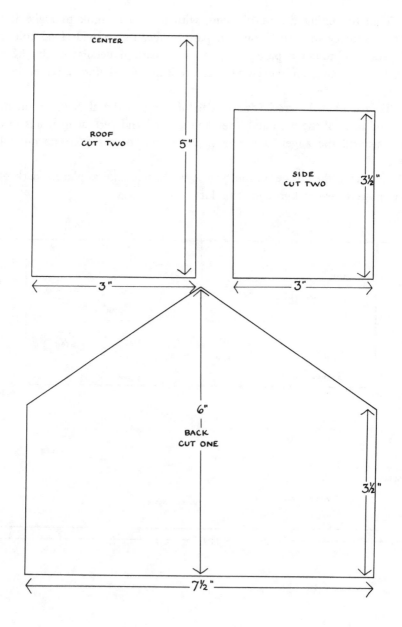

CENTER

ROOF
CUT TWO   5"

3"

SIDE
CUT TWO   3½"

3"

6"

BACK
CUT ONE

3½"

7½"

HANSEL AND GRETEL'S GINGERBREAD HOUSE

A spiced roll-out cookie dough
(see pages 166 and 167)
Confectioners' sugar for
decorator's icing
Tiny marshmallows
Small gumdrops

Cinnamon red-hots
Candied cherries
Small assorted candies
Shredded coconut
Food colors

The gingerbread house is constructed in very much the same way as the cookie crèche but it's easier to make and less time-consuming. When finished, it is perfectly enchanting. Every child should have one at Christmastime.

Make one of the spiced roll-out doughs and refrigerate. Work with a small portion of the dough at a time, keeping the rest chilled.

Roll out dough on a lightly floured surface about ⅛ inch thick. Note the dimensions of the patterns shown on pages 198–199 and, using a ruler and a sharp knife, cut out the base on which the house will sit, and the two sections of the roof. Carefully transfer these parts to an oiled baking sheet by rolling them over the rolling pin, picking up both rolling pin and dough and unrolling the dough on the baking sheet. Square up the sides and corners with the side of the ruler. Bake according to recipe directions, being careful not to let the cookies overbrown. Cool on the baking sheet for a few minutes, then shift each piece around a little with a spatula to make sure it doesn't stick to the baking sheet.

While still warm, cut tiny slots in the base where you are going to set the trees and Hansel and Gretel.

Roll out another portion of the dough and, following the dimensions, cut out the front, back, and the two sides.

Cut out trees, steps, Hansel and Gretel, and the witch with her broom and cat. (These figures won't need to be enlarged if you've followed the dimensions given for the house itself.) Transfer the cut-outs to an oiled baking sheet with a wide spatula and make sure the corners of the front and sides are square and the little figures are not out of shape.

With a sharp knife, score the dough deeply where the windows and doors will be. Bake and cool, but while still warm cut through the dough, separating the doors and windows from the front and sides. Let the gingerbread cool completely and become crisp before icing and decorating it.

Before assembling the house, the roof and walls are spread with decorator's icing. The icing should be smooth and thin enough to spread easily without running. Ice the doors and window cut-outs, too. Spread the trees with green icing and "dress" the figures of Hansel and Gretel with colored icing pressed through a pastry tube fitted with a small plain tube. Let the icing dry thoroughly.

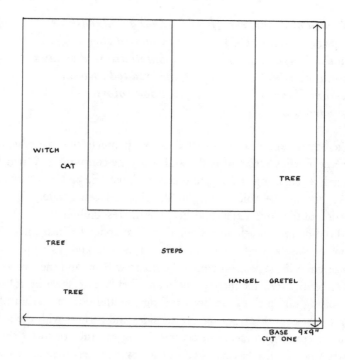

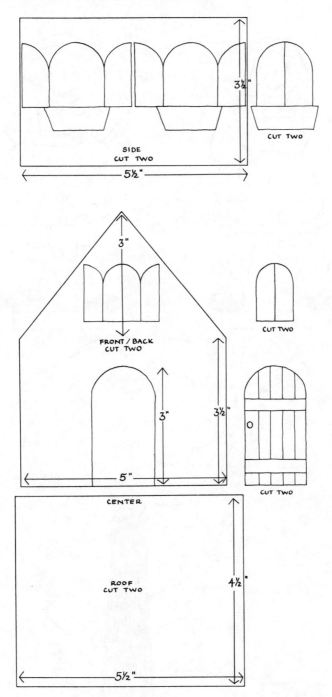

SIDE
CUT TWO

3½"

5½"

CUT TWO

3"

FRONT / BACK
CUT TWO

CUT TWO

3½"

3"

5"

CENTER

O

CUT TWO

ROOF
CUT TWO

4½"

5½"

Assembling the House: Set the base of the house on a tray so it can be moved from kitchen to mantlepiece or table. Spread the bottom edge and sides of the back of the house with thick confectioners' icing and center it close to the back edge of the base. Prop it with toothpicks and attach the sides and front in the same way. Let the "glue" dry thoroughly before attaching the roof with decorator's icing and toothpicks. Remove the toothpicks when the "glue" sets.

Attach the doors by their "hinges"; cut the squares removed from the sides and front of the house for windows in half and "glue" on either side of the windows for shutters. Set the steps leading up to the front door in place.

Decorating the House: Dip one end of the tiny marshmallows into decorator's icing and use them as studs all down the edges of the house where two of the sections meet and under the eaves where the roof meets the sides. Decorate the sides, front, and roof with gumdrops, candied cherries, and other small candies, "gluing" them on in the same way. Use half a candied cherry for each door knob.

Set the trees, Hansel and Gretel, and the witch and cat in their slots with a dab of icing; sprinkle the base with shredded coconut and add some gumdrops or a pile of marshmallows here and there. Drop some small candies on a pathway leading to the front door, for the pebbles that Hansel dropped.

NOTE: If your gingerbread house is to be a mantlepiece decoration or will be sitting under a chandelier or near a window frame, you may wish to suspend, cookiemobile fashion, some clouds, stars, and a moon over the house and set a dark night-blue background behind it.

AND LAST BUT NOT LEAST, LET THERE BE POPCORN . . .

. . . big bowls of buttered popcorn, garlands of the stark-white kernels alternating with bright red shiny cranberries to drape the tree, and let there be popcorn balls to eat and to hang from the branches. Make the balls large or miniature. When dry, wrap each in transparent film, twisting the top to close it and tying it with Christmas ribbon.

POPCORN BALLS

12 cups freshly popped corn　　　*3 cups brown sugar*
Salt to taste　　　　　　　　　　*¾ cup water*
3 tablespoons butter

Put popped corn in a large container and sprinkle lightly with salt.

In heavy saucepan melt butter, add brown sugar, and water and cook, stirring, until sugar is dissolved. Then bring to a boil and boil without stirring until the syrup reaches the soft-ball stage (326°). Pour syrup over the popcorn, stirring gently, until each kernel is coated with the syrup.

Flour hands lightly and shape the popcorn mixture into balls. Work quickly and handle the corn gently. Put balls on waxed paper to cool and dry.
Makes 12 3-inch balls.

TINY TUTTI-FRUITY POPCORN BALLS

10 cups freshly popped corn　　　*⅔ cup light corn syrup*
1 6-ounce can pecan halves　　　*2 tablespoons water*
1 4-ounce jar candied red cherries,　*16 large marshmallows (¼ pound)*
　halved　　　　　　　　　　　*½ teaspoon peppermint extract*
1 pound confectioners' sugar

In 2 buttered jelly roll pans mix popcorn, pecans, and cherries.

In a saucepan combine 1 cup of the sugar, the corn syrup, and water. Bring to a boil over low heat, stirring until sugar is dissolved, then stir in remaining sugar and bring to a boil. Stir in marshmallows and continue to stir until marshmallows are melted. Remove from heat and stir in the peppermint extract.

Pour half the syrup over popcorn mixture in each pan and toss evenly until well coated. Cool until easy to handle, then shape into 1½-inch balls. Let stand on waxed paper until firm. Store in a tightly covered container.

Makes 1 dozen popcorn balls.

Metric Equivalent Chart

LENGTH

1 inch (in)	=	2.5 centimeters (cm)
1 foot (ft)	=	30 centimeters (cm)
1 millimeter (mm)	=	.04 inches (in)
1 centimeter (cm)	=	.4 inches (in)
1 meter (m)	=	3.3 feet (ft)

MASS WEIGHT

1 ounce (oz)	=	28 grams (g)
1 pound (lb)	=	450 grams (g)
1 gram (g)	=	.035 ounces (oz)
1 kilogram (kg) or 1000 g	=	2.2 pounds (lbs)

LIQUID VOLUME

1 fluid ounce (fl. oz)	=	30 milliliters (ml)
1 fluid cup (c)	=	240 milliliters (ml)
1 pint (pt)	=	470 milliliters (ml)
1 quart (qt)	=	950 milliliters (ml)
1 gallon (gal)	=	3.8 liters (l)
1 milliliter (ml)	=	.03 fluid ounces (fl. oz)
1 liter (l) or 1000 ml	=	2.1 fluid pints or 1.06 fluid quarts
1 liter (l)	=	.26 gallons (gal)

Index

205